Unashamed Servant-Leadership, authored
leader Rachel R. Rajagopal, is a unique s
myriad others, who have undergone painful and humbling experiences in
their commitment to Christian service. The socio-cultural settings, gender
prejudices and theological context of Asia quite often limit the growth of Asian
women leaders to their fullest potential. The author's well-researched work is
a great combination of rich theology, missiology, presentation and analysis
of facts. Above all, what she writes arises from her real-life experience and
is exemplified in her life and service. The book is deeply insightful and has
uncommon content with academic rigor. I am sure that this book will be a
valuable asset to the Asian Christian community and, in particular, a great
inspiration to the Christian women of Asia. It's a must-read!

Sundar Sangma
Vice President, International Ministry Development, Haggai Institute

Dr Rachel Rajagopal's book, *Unashamed Servant-Leadership*, was birthed from
her personal background, secular work experience and Christian ministry
involvement. Despite all odds, first as a female, then as an Indian growing up in
a Hindu environment, and serving God as a female missionary in Asia, Africa,
Latin America and beyond, the author has overcome numerous challenges to
become one of Asia's few women who dare to be different and are "unashamed"
to be God's leaders! What is most powerful in this book are the snapshots of
ten women from different ethnic, social, educational, and single and marital
backgrounds, from different countries, including the Middle East, all of whom
have risen under different and difficult situations to take on leadership, and,
in the process, blossomed and thrived as God's servant-leaders. I trust that
many will read this book and that the stories of these daughters of Asia will
bless men and women, and give courage especially to Asian women to rise up
and let God use them for his kingdom work and his greater glory.

Violet James, PhD
Chaplain, Singapore Bible College, Singapore

It is about time that we heard the voices of Asian Christian women servant-leaders. We need to understand, be increasingly aware of, and recognize their contribution in national, regional, and global leadership contexts.

This book is a must-read! It provides a comprehensive discussion and encourages the Asian Church to release and acknowledge the gifted women who serve alongside men servant-leaders.

Sierry Tendero, EdD
Adviser, Philippine Council of Evangelical Churches (PCEC) Women's Commission
Missions Director, Kamuning Bible Christian Fellowship, Quezon City, Philippines

If you are expecting *Unashamed Servant-Leadership* to provide pat answers to the perplexing problem of the lack of Asian Christian women in leadership, look elsewhere. Writing from an insider's perspective, Rajagopal crafts a much-needed start to the discussion of inequality. The uniquely prepared author invites ten daughters of Asia, operating from a culture of shame, to unashamedly tell their real-life narratives of transformation and encouragement despite Christian leadership revolving around men. In the light of cultural, spiritual, familial, theological and other challenges inherent in Asian societies, the forum of female voices and the author's insightful interpretations challenge the church to mobilize and activate Asian Christian women into servant-leadership. As the Majority World church continues to swell, *Unashamed Servant-Leadership* is an important addition to leadership and missional libraries.

Karen Hatley, PhD
Professor, Missional Leadership, Missional University, North Augusta, SC, USA
Author of *Missionaries from Everywhere to Everywhere: A Delphi Study to Identify the Emerging Roles of US Missionaries in the Majority World*

Global Perspectives Series

Unashamed
Servant-Leadership

GLOBAL LIBRARY

Unashamed Servant-Leadership

Rachel R. Rajagopal

GLOBAL LIBRARY

© 2017 by Rachel R. Rajagopal

Published 2017 by Langham Global Library
An imprint of Langham Creative Projects

Langham Partnership
PO Box 296, Carlisle, Cumbria CA3 9WZ, UK
www.langham.org

Isbns:
978-1-78368-366-6 Print
978-1-78368-367-3 Epub
978-1-78368-368-0 Mobi
978-1-78368-369-7 PDF

Rachel R. Rajagopal has asserted her right under the Copyright, Designs and Patents Act, 1988 to be identified as the Author of this work.

All rights reserved. No part of this publication may be reproduced, stored in a retrieval system or transmitted, in any form or by any means, electronic, mechanical, photocopying, recording or otherwise, without the prior written permission of the publisher or the Copyright Licensing Agency.

Unless otherwise indicated, Scripture quotations are from The Holy Bible, English Standard Version˚ (ESV˚), copyright © 2001 by Crossway, a publishing ministry of Good News Publishers. Used by permission. All rights reserved.

British Library Cataloguing in Publication Data
A catalogue record for this book is available from the British Library

ISBN: 978-1-78368-366-6

Cover & Book Design: projectluz.com

Langham Partnership actively supports theological dialogue and an author's right to publish but does not necessarily endorse the views and opinions set forth here or in works referenced within this publication, nor can we guarantee technical and grammatical correctness. Langham Partnership does not accept any responsibility or liability to persons or property as a consequence of the reading, use or interpretation of its published content.

Dedication

To all Christian leaders, both men and women, who continue to release women into servant-leadership so that
we might together bring great glory to our God

CONTENTS

Preface

I have been involved in intercultural missions since 1995. That is a long enough time to have come to some conclusions about the challenges faced by Asian Christian women servant-leaders. As an Asian Christian female missions leader, I have faced challenges in my own leadership growth – at every turn and at every corner. They were painful and humbling experiences.

Thus, when I began to write my doctoral dissertation, I desired to know if other Asian Christian women leaders had faced challenges to their growth as ministry leaders, and their manner of overcoming these challenges.

This book is an attempt to communicate to readers that Asian Christian women servant-leaders with evangelical beliefs lack any real "voice" in the Asian Christian community. We will hear the voices of ten Asian Christian women who are speaking together in order that their collective voice might be heard and recognized. These servant-leaders offered their voices by sharing their encounters with Jesus and their personal obedience to God's call despite challenges to their growth as ministry leaders. These voices belong to Asian Christian women who are truly Asian – born in Asia, primarily educated in Asia and still living and ministering in Asia. Their stories concerning their spiritual birth, calling into ministry, growth as ministry leaders and the challenges that accompanied their growth are told here. Each leader's response reflects her personal understanding and experiences, which were shaped by her social, cultural and theological context.

One of the discoveries I made as I listened to these Asian voices is that moral encouragement from both male and female Christian leaders was highly valued and much needed as these Christian women grew and served in their leadership responsibilities. Especially, they desired the moral encouragement of male Christian leaders as a sign of acknowledgment and acceptance of equality in leadership. The support from their male loved ones – fathers, brothers, husbands, sons – and from the men in their churches and congregations, especially pastors, was valuable. However, in most cases, the women's social, cultural and theological contexts did not allow for moral encouragement and acknowledgment or acceptance of their positions as servant-leaders in the Christian community. These women encountered hindrances that made their leadership journey more difficult than it would be for their male counterparts. During these times, other women in these Asian churches and congregations rallied around them with verbal encouragements and prayer support.

Acknowledgments

I thank God for allowing me to go through interesting challenges as I have walked the path of servant-leadership. I have been blessed to experience his faithfulness as well as his sufficient grace during moments of weakness. I will be eternally grateful for this experience of learning from outstanding men and women in the process: like most Asians, my family, friends and teachers matter to me. But first, all glory goes to the Lord Jesus Christ – without him, I am nothing.

Their lack of formal education did not stop my parents, Rajagopal and Saroja, from sending their four girls to school. My three younger sisters, Chitra, Vasantha and Banu, are collectively an inspiration for their lifelong learning attitudes. My brothers-in-law, Dr Peter Hugger and Warrant Officer Sivakumar, are men of excellence who practice equality in marriage. My five nieces (Charmaine, Nadhia, Verena, Victoria and Thhivya) and only nephew (Andreas) continue to remind me that gender equality tensions continue to exist minimally for millennials. Though there are more women than men in my family home in Singapore, there is a sense of respect and equality among us regardless of gender, ethnicity, nationality and some cultural and age differences. Difference in religious beliefs has not diluted our respect towards each other as individuals with diverse talents.

I am especially thankful to the women who freely shared their narratives and to many friends who have encouraged me with moral and prayer support at different junctures of this writing journey.

List of Tables and Map

1

Self-Retrospection: Being an Asian, Female and Servant-Leader in the Christian Environment

I have a sense that most men and women might say "Why not?" to the question "Can Asian Christian women be ministry leaders?" But is this thought or verbal response the general reality in the Asian Church?[1]

The small number of Asian women authors and global leaders inspired my own curiosity. I prayerfully embarked on the sensitive issue of Asian women in Christian leadership. My own struggles to be accepted as a servant of Christ capable of leading both men and women were a mild "push" factor. I wondered if other Asian women struggled to exercise their leadership gifts. Were Asian Christian women limited in their service as leaders to a particular group – for example, serving by leading groups of women, youth or children? Were Asian Christian women leaders limited to teaching those younger than them? Or were they free to exercise leadership beyond their local/national church boundaries regardless of gender, age differences or multicultural contexts?

I come from a minority ethnic group on the small island of Singapore. In Singapore, four religions, ethnicities and languages are officially recognized even though we are a nation with cultural and linguistic diversity. My own family has had a mixture of social, cultural and ethnic backgrounds since the time of my grandparents: a Straits-born Chinese grandmother, an Indian

---

1. Church with a capital "C" is a reference to the global evangelical Church, while church with a lower-case "c" refers to the local evangelical church.

grandmother, an Indian grandfather who was a chauffeur and another Indian grandfather who ran a small business. My immediate and extended family includes Europeans and Eurasians. Despite different educational levels, extended family members have held good jobs. My three younger sisters and I were strongly encouraged by our paternal uncles to be independent and to study well. My sisters and I studied hard, worked hard, continue to support our parents and enjoy our togetherness – albeit in a non-Christian environment.

As I was the firstborn of four daughters, my parents used to joke that I was the "son" in the family. I grew up challenging the norms and standards of Hindu cultural practices and became a "secret Christian" in secondary school. This secrecy allowed me to behave in ungodly ways that often elicited a false repentance. The lingering awareness of my inappropriate carnality became a conscious realization when I was discipled for a year, in 1994, by a Singaporean Chinese doctor, Dr Raymond Teo, almost fifteen years after my initial "acceptance" of salvation. I realized that, while I had an understanding of the gospel, I had not exercised intellectual, emotional and volitional commitment to Christ; Jesus Christ of Nazareth was not the Lord of my life.

After I repented and determined that Christ must be first and foremost in my life, God put me on a fast track of spiritual growth. The fast-track growth was painful: humbling myself over and over again in order to do what was right before God was not my cup of tea! Yet there was a sense of peace in the journey with Christ.

As a member of the minority Indian group in Singapore, I had made it a personal life goal to "make it" and "be somebody"; this personal and worldly ambition consumed me until God called me out, retrained me and gave me ambitions covered by his grace, righteousness and favor while immersed in the love of Christ. A transformation within me through the power of the Holy Spirit and a deep-seated certainty of a specific calling launched me into missionary work in 1996. I was called to global missions in early 1997 and, in due course, God would be specific as to how I was to impact lives.

Prior to my call to servant-leadership in global missions, my employers often gave me pioneering positions and responsibilities. Being the firstborn, I had already had the responsibility to care for my siblings. I became an "accidental" leader during my last year of pre-university when I was elected the president of the literary, debate and drama society. At Singapore Bible College, I ended up being the vice-president for the Graduation Organizing Committee.

Though I had many pioneering opportunities in various professions, I learned most about leadership when God provided me with the privilege of serving in the Singapore Armed Forces as a lieutenant. During my time with the defense force, I held various appointments that demanded my time and commitment. I served with and was led by very capable male leaders who allowed me to grow under their leadership.

Later, I served with foreign male employers who also gave me leadership opportunities at departmental as well as regional levels. These professional engagements in challenging company activities with mostly male colleagues were in secular contexts; gender, ethnicity, culture or nationality were never issues to my growth in leadership.

In 1991, I began to attend a local Christian church that supported ordained female pastors. However, it was in the church context that I began to feel and sense the inequality. In most of the churches that I visited or attended, there were few women in leadership appointments, and yet I interacted with so many gifted women in the respective congregations. Few women preached on Sundays at the main services. Was it because they were not gifted preachers – or was there a silent rule about women not being recognized as leaders, teachers and preachers in some Christian churches? Why were there so few women in church executive teams?

After I joined a worldwide mission organization in 2002, I began to work in diverse cultural and national contexts. I truly believe in the Great Commission:

> And Jesus came and said to them, "All authority in heaven and on earth has been given to me. Go therefore and make disciples of all nations, baptizing them in the name of the Father and of the Son and of the Holy Spirit, teaching them to observe all that I have commanded you. And behold, I am with you always, to the end of the age." (Matt 28:18–20)

Everywhere I travelled in the mission fields to teach pastors and leaders, men would be the largest group in my class. Women's participation in discipleship classes was negligible. Once when I travelled to the Middle East to teach an inductive Bible study course, I discovered that the leaders had expected a male teacher. In Nepal, the all-male group of rural pastors tested my knowledge of the Bible for forty-five minutes before they accepted me as their sister in Christ and their facilitator, teaching them the basics of discipleship. As recently as 2016, a Christian brother sent to meet me at the airport completely missed me because he was expecting a male leader to arrive for a conference which had an all-male attendance.

In all my discipleship classes, the few women who joined learned so well that I could see the transformation in their thoughts and actions. All the women I have ever discipled used the same course materials and were given the same assignments as men – they were not given preferential treatment – and they proved that they were able to think as well as their brothers in Christ. In fact, some of the best students were actually women who were not ordained pastors. Just like their brothers in Christ, the women's goal was to obey God and to use their gifts accordingly. These were true evangelical Christians who desired to be obedient to the Lord Jesus Christ.

In the course of ministry, I have met Christian brothers who acknowledged me as leader and honored me for serving God faithfully. I have also met Christian brothers who have questioned my leadership, especially frowning on the possibility of establishing a new missions agency, preaching from the pulpit or travelling to various nations as a single woman to teach pastors and church leaders. The latter challenges have not stopped in the twenty-first century, unfortunately.

Life Narratives with a Purpose

In order to discern the growth in ministry leadership of Asian Christian women servant-leaders, and the opportunities and challenges they have encountered, we need to listen to their life narratives. Our life narratives are powerful and allow us to understand self and others. I do assume that there is a theologically justifiable place for biblically educated and Christ-centered Asian women as servant-leaders in the various arenas of God's kingdom and the evangelical community.

The ten narratives in this book engage with (1) the influence of Asian contexts in shaping opportunities and challenges; (2) their awareness of biblical principles of servant-leadership; (3) their development as leaders in their Christian environment; and (4) the opportunities and challenges for these Asian Christian women developing as servant-leaders.

There are no comparisons of leadership styles between Asian Christian men and women in this book. Rather, I am concerned with the challenges encountered by Asian Christian women servant-leaders, their perspectives of Christian leadership, and their experiences and approaches to various challenges in primarily male-dominated cultural contexts.

The insights gained from the narratives of these twenty-first-century women will be beneficial in mobilizing Asian Christian women into servant-leadership and encouraging Asian Christian male servant-leaders to release gifted women into leadership. I hope that, together, we will be able to see the similarities or the differences and begin to adjust our approaches to empowering and releasing gifted women into their God-given roles and responsibilities, without fear or favor.

These evangelical Christian women are from nations such as India, Jordan, Malaysia, Singapore and South Korea. They are educated, well-travelled and from the middle-class social strata. All of them are actively involved in national, regional and global mission ministries. As these women do not represent all Asian Christian women from various ethnicities or nationalities, educational backgrounds, religious affiliations or social statuses, some of the opportunities identified in the interviewees' life narratives may not apply to other Asian Christian women. Due to the implications of socio-cultural differences and contexts, non-Asians, Asians who are naturalized citizens of non-Asian countries or Asians who have spent their formative developmental years in non-Asian countries may respond differently.

There are various scriptural and theological understandings regarding the leadership roles available to men and women in church and family. While we will briefly review the complementarian and egalitarian perspectives on male/female leadership and some of the newer perspectives from feminist theology, it is not my purpose to develop a theology of church leadership. There are extensive writings on the theology of church leadership. Rather, my purpose is to provide a voice, through the use of narrative methodology, for Asian Christian women servant-leaders who are engaged in ministry.

Summary

Personal curiosity and the need to provide a louder voice for Asian Christian women servant-leaders gave birth to this book. The ten narratives in this book reveal transformational experiences that are meant to enable readers to "hear" their voices and engage with the experiences of these women. These testimonies of contemporary Asian Christian women pursuing servant-leadership in a male hierarchical context will serve as an encouragement to the Asian Church and especially to emerging Asian Christian women servant-leaders. I hope that readers will be challenged by the transformational lives of these modern-day apostles, prophets, evangelists, pastors and teachers (Eph 4:11). These twenty-first-century women have been placed in communities and nations to foster lifestyles that will glorify God (Matt 5:16).

We step beyond understanding to increase our own awareness and to recognize the contributions of Asian Christian women servant-leaders in national, regional and global servant-leadership contexts. Your personal discovery and recognition of their challenges will be key for nurturing, rethinking and building effective Christian ministry.

2

The Lack of Voice among Asian Christian Women Servant-Leaders

Few Asian Christian women servant-leaders have publicly shared their personal Christian life and leadership growth and there continues to be a dearth of records of their experiences in and for Asian Christian Church history. However, the political and corporate leadership of many Christian and non-Christian Asian women is duly recognized in literature and the media. For example, we are generally aware of the experiences of the late Prime Minister Indira Gandhi of India, nineteenth-century Indian Brahmin convert to Christianity Pandita Ramabai, and Myanmarese politician Aung San Suu Kyi. While we have observed the rise of Asian women leaders in the corporate world, we have yet to see the significant rise of Asian women in Christian leadership in this century.

We are thankful for the insights from Western perspectives in all areas of theology and missiology. Asian nations would not have received the gospel of Jesus Christ if not for the arrival of Western missionaries and their offer of education, healthcare, social welfare and other services. What these missionaries began continues to bear fruit even today. In fact, we have taken some of these ideas to other shores and seen a greater impact for the kingdom of God.

Asian Christian men such as Watchman Nee, revivalist John Sung of China, Reverend Ha Young Jo of South Korea, Bishop Robert Solomon of Singapore and Dhinakaran of India are among those who have been or still are visible as authors, preachers and theologians; extremely few Asian Christian women leaders have had the same recognition or visibility for their journeys in the kingdom; the voices of Asian Christian women leaders are rarely acknowledged or heard. It is not uncommon for us to whisper our thoughts and nod our heads for the sake of Christian unity. Let us not rock the boat with heavy theology! In addition, I know of Asian Christian women-pastor friends who work harder than their male counterparts but receive a lower wage than them. Do you ever wonder why there is such a discrepancy in a Christian environment?

Out of curiosity, I did a quick word search on the word "women" in a prominent Bible college library based in Singapore in April 2006. It yielded 168 entries. Only three authors were women of Asian background or had Asian-sounding names. Another search at the same library in October 2010 yielded 379 entries. At least thirteen authors were women of Asian background or had Asian-sounding names. A third search in June 2012 yielded 446 entries. Twenty-one authors were women of Asian background or had Asian-sounding names. While there has been a substantial increase in the catalogued library books related to women between 2006 and 2012, books by women of Asian background or with Asian-sounding names remain a very small percentage of the total in this category (women): 1.7 percent in 2006; 4.7 percent in 2012.

In 2009, I sent a brief one-question electronic mail survey to forty highly experienced Asian Christian women servant-leaders from India, Indonesia, Korea and the Philippines asking if they had read about any Asian Christian women leaders who have made an impact on society and are considered Christian role models. Twenty of the forty women responded. Fifteen of them (75 percent) replied with a resounding "No." Five women mentioned that they had come across testimonies of Asian Christian women; only two women had actually read about an Asian Christian woman leader: Gulshan Esther Fatima.[1] One Asian Christian woman remarked, "I have yet to read about any Asian Christian women leaders. Come to think of it – where are they?" The fact that articles or writings pertaining to Asian Christian women are even smaller in number serves as an indication that the voice of Asian Christian women, and especially leaders, remains subdued.

---

1. Gulshan was born in Pakistan to a wealthy family. In 1952 she was crippled by a sickness contracted at birth. She yearned to discover the truth and after her father's death she searched the Urdu Qur'an for Jesus. Over a long period, she asked Jesus for healing. Finally, he appeared in her room, healed her and commanded her to be a witness to his people. She suffered much for her unshakeable faith. After travelling to England and Canada to witness to Christ, she took up residence in England (Gulshan and Sangster, *The Torn Veil*).

Possible Negative Effects of Culture and Traditions

In September 2010, I relocated to Seoul, South Korea, and assumed my new responsibilities as Director for the Overseas Ministry Division at my former mission organization. My work responsibilities included writing policies, restructuring the division, overseeing global operations and discipleship of church pastors and leaders among the nations under my portfolio. As part of restructuring the division, I invited suitable volunteers to take on the leadership of the four departments; two Korean women who had exhibited godliness in character and leadership qualities were invited to take up the headship of two departments.

One invitee, a single associate pastor, promptly replied that she was not able to handle "such a big task." She later acknowledged that it was wrong of her to think that the task was "too big" for her and that her dependence "on God's grace" and to "approach it joyfully" would have been the right response. Unfortunately, this transformational revelation did not translate into acceptance of the invitation.

The other South Korean invitee, the regional manager for an American entity, was excited about the prospect of leading the new department but wished to pray with her husband before accepting my invitation; the next day, she called to inform me that she was "not qualified" for the headship of the department, and added that she was needed at home. Her initial blazing enthusiasm and very positive attitude did not translate to action after praying with her husband.

Another female Asian pastor, also a good disciple of Christ and a disciple-maker, was invited to help with a new discipleship project. Her prompt response was: "if you think I am qualified."

A Socio-Cultural Headache?

Admittedly, the above responses do not constitute proof of a cultural suppression of Asian Christian women servant-leaders. It is conceivable that male leaders (whether Asian or Western) may doubt their own capacities and that, in some church contexts in the West, some women's responses might be inhibited by their church or family culture. As these encounters are, in my view, artifacts of a culture of suppression that is far more pronounced in Asia than elsewhere, they raise the following questions about the disposition of Asian Christian women servant-leaders and their voices:

- Why are Asian Christian women servant-leaders' voices just a whisper in the Church?
- Why would a pastor who leads a congregation assume that she might not be qualified to be a disciple-maker at a regional or global level?
- Why do some Asian Christian women servant-leaders think that certain tasks are "too big" for them?
- What is the role of Christian husbands in their wives' decision-making process – especially if their wives are invited to take on leadership appointments?
- Why would some Asian Christian women servant-leaders state and sense that they might not be qualified for certain tasks?
- How can Asian Christian women servant-leaders' voices progress from a whisper to a firm assertive voice in the kingdom of God?

As I listened to some Asian Christian women tell their own stories of salvation, discover their own freedom and potential as servant-leaders in ministry and reflect on who or what supported or hindered their service as leaders in ministry, I asked myself these questions of current and emerging Asian Christian women servant-leaders:

- Do they deeply know the liberating power of the gospel and the freedom of transformation that it brings to them?
- Are they restricted in practicing this liberating and transforming power of the gospel? Who or what is restricting them?

One question that kept pounding my mind like a headache was: why does it seem an embarrassment, even shameful, to serve Christ using the leadership gift that God has given the Asian Christian women?

I never really thought that a shame culture operated among confident Asian Christian women. But there it was – like a thorn in the flesh. It was almost an apology for being strong, capable and humble servant-leaders, as if it was their fault for being all that they could be in the Lord Jesus Christ.

Understanding Asian Society and Women

In order to understand the majority of Asian women, one needs to unveil the curtains of Asian society. Asia's contradictions permeate the Christian community. One such contradiction is related to the undeniable impact of Asian women as pioneers and servant-leaders in ministry against the continuing reality that the voices of Asian Christian women are unrecognized or unheard.

Asia: A Paradoxical Society

Paradox abounds in daily life in Asia. Asia surges with economic opportunities; Asia is also immersed in poverty. Though Asia comes across as somewhat modern, the *purdah*[2] of traditional philosophies and rules and regulations govern many aspects of Asian societies: Asia's traditions, rules and regulations remain implicit and veiled.

Asian Population: Female Workforce

Asia accounts for slightly more than half of the current world population, estimated at 7.37 billion.[3] Out of the estimated 4.3 billion Asians,[4] around 2.2 billion are female.[5] Asian women and girls thus make up close to 30 percent of the world's population.

Jane Horan, founder of a Singapore consultancy focusing on developing Asian women leaders, claimed in a *Bloomberg Business Week* report that Asian women will soon be a major source of talent in the workforce.[6] Horan observes that Asian women are increasingly well qualified, and "well-educated, multilingual and assuredly driven."[7] Asian women leaders will be transformational and will contribute to the extraordinary performance of any organization.[8]

According to the 2010 United Nations Educational, Scientific and Cultural Organization (UNESCO) *Global Education Digest* report, among Asian nations, at least 50 percent of the student population pursuing a bachelor's degree were women and "women are more likely than men to pursue their second degree."[9] Tertiary education is increasing in the majority of developing nations in Asia, and women are more likely to complete a higher degree. When this

---

2. *Purdah* is a Persian word for "curtain" or "veil." It is essentially a cloth covering the whole body of women in Hindu or Muslim societies so that their bodies remain hidden before men or strangers. The word is also used to refer to women in these societies living in a separate room or behind a curtain so that strangers and men, other than immediate family members, will not have any access to them.

3. United States Census Bureau.

4. United Nations ESCAP, *2016 ESCAP Population Data Sheet.*

5. United Nations Population Division, "WPP2015 POP."

6. Horan, "How to Retain," para. 3.

7. Horan, para. 3.

8. Horan, para. 4.

9. UNESCO Institute for Statistics, *Global Education Digest 2010,* 68–79.

report is linked to the proportion of the world's population comprising around 2.2 billion Asian women and Horan's argument, the implication is that an increasing proportion of the Asian and global workforce – and possibly those in leadership – will be educated Asian women. The Christian community in Asia will not be exempt from this extension of educated, hardworking Asian Christian women.

Asian Business Neighborhood: Poverty, Wealth, Corruption and Innovation

One Asian paradox is related to the multibillion-dollar beauty industry that presents "heavenly"[10] retreats and spas to soothe the mind, body and soul. This co-exists with the filth, slums and the effects of natural disasters.[11] Prasso cites Professor Gerard Bodeker's observation that there is "a huge awareness in global value and interest in Asian therapies, [and] so Asian countries are now actively discovering and promoting their own health and heritage."[12] Only three years earlier, an Asia-Pacific Ministerial Conference on Housing and Human Settlements report stated that Asia had the largest share of slums and almost one billion people dwelt in the slums of Asia.[13]

Though Asian nations continue to boast about their super business hubs and the ultimate comforts in airport lounges, Asia is also known for corruption in the highest official echelons that results in protests, riots and suicides. Human and sex trafficking including prostitution, pedophilia, child labor and child marriages are examples of corrupt practices generating billion-dollar businesses in Asia. An article in *Bloomberg Business Week* mentioned that the governments of Singapore, South Korea and Japan support innovative business practices,[14] and Singapore is identified as the best Asian city for venture companies[15] and the "least corrupted" Asian country among the top

---

10. The word "heavenly" is used here to depict the peacefulness and relaxation that spas promote.

11. The phrase "filth, slums and effects of natural disasters" reminds one of the filth easily associated with slum areas in Bangladesh, India, Indonesia, Pakistan, Thailand; disasters such as the pandemic illnesses in China, Singapore, Taiwan; floods and volcanic eruptions in the Philippines and the devastating tsunami of 2006 which affected many countries including South Asian countries.

12. Prasso, "Spas Take Off," para. 6.

13. UN-Habitat, "Asia-Pacific Ministerial Conference," 2.

14. Einhorn, "Innovation," para. 2.

15. McCullum, "VCs Say."

ten countries in the world.[16] Yet journalist Veronica Uy states that a growing number of Filipino women have been "lured to Singapore on the false promise of a high-paying job only to end up in prostitution."[17]

Success and Suppression: Status of Women and Children in Asian Societies

Despite the suppression, mistreatment and even trafficking of Asian women, Asian countries continue to produce female heads of state. Bangladesh, China, India, Indonesia, Israel, Kyrgyzstan, Mongolia, the Philippines, Singapore, South Korea, Sri Lanka and Thailand have all had at least one female head of state.[18] The success in producing female heads of state does not diminish suppression in the form of female infanticide and child marriages especially enforced on girls. Violence and lack of basic human rights are still ongoing issues in parts of Asia in this twenty-first century.

Another form of suppression is seen in the denial of education to children. For example, the Taliban shot Malala Yousafzai, a young Muslim girl,[19] when she championed the cause for every Pakistani child to receive education. Chaudhry's recent Reuters article demonstrates that millions of Pakistani children are forced to work due to the country's economic pressures.[20]

In an online article concerned with critical issues facing women due to the global gender imbalance, Columbia University Professor Lena Edlunds warned:

> The introduction of fertility technology made sex selection much easier, but it is the cultural norms and the willingness to reject a female child that mattered most. The trend is no longer just confined to India and China. Increasing sex ratio imbalances are showing up in South Korea, Taiwan, Vietnam, Albania, Armenia and other Caucasus countries . . . The male perspective is that there aren't enough women to marry or have as a partner. The female perspective is lost because, for women, the problem is they are becoming reduced to a chattel being produced by [the] poor and sold to the richer male population.[21]

---

16. Transparency International, "Corruption Perceptions Index 2011."
17. Uy, "Trafficking," para. 5.
18. Center for Asia-Pacific Women in Politics, "Women Heads of State."
19. Stableford, "Malala Yousafzai."
20. Chaudhry, "Millions Pushed."
21. Panagoda, "Global Gender Imbalance," paras. 8–9.

This was further affirmed, in the same article, by the US Department of State's 2009 *Trafficking in Persons* report: "widening gender imbalance in Asia as a cause of increased sex trafficking [and] trends are increasing in Asia for forced marriages, forced prostitution, and trans-border marriages where women in poor areas are married off to men in richer regions."[22]

While there are many Asian women in senior leadership or in top management positions in the corporate world, there are even more Asian women being trafficked and forced into prostitution. Young Asian girls are forced into marriage and denied education. In places like India, Eve-teasing,[23] molestation and gang-rapes are shamefully common.

Cultural and Religious Portraits of Asian Women

The tensions relating to modern Asian women's roles in traditional society are highlighted by thirteen female researchers belonging to the Women Caucus of the Asian Studies Association of Australia in *Women in Asia: Tradition, Modernity and Globalization*.[24] They address the tension in women's roles in the following areas: between modernity and tradition; status of women; impact of globalization and consumerism; disagreements between national culture and Western feminism; and the impact of governmental influence on sexual health, contraception and family size.

The ten women who share their narratives in this book are individuals bound by a commonality: they are all Asians who address the tension of cultural traditions and modern societal acceptance, and their different roles as a Christian daughter, wife, mother and servant-leader actively serving the Lord Jesus Christ. Their narratives share common ground: their gender, Christian faith in an Asian society and interactions with a conglomeration of groups, cultures, languages and gods; these experiences are challenges as well as learning experiences.

Perceptions of Being Women in Asia

In their review of research between 1970 and 2000, Roces and Edwards affirmed that though an Asian woman does not belong to a homogeneous

---

22. Panagoda, paras. 8–9.

23. "Eve-teasing" is slang used in India, Bangladesh and Pakistan to denote sexual harassment and molestation of women by men.

24. Roces and Edwards, "Contesting Gender Narratives."

community, "the modern Asian woman exudes contradiction and ambivalence as she straddles between tradition and modernity, victimization and agency, between being a subject and an object . . ."[25]

In her article "Contextualizing Asian Theologies: Women's Perspectives,"[26] Hnuni cites Rebecca Moon's observation that Korean women "have been denied recognition of their dignity and equality with all men. This is largely as a result of an unjust and exploitative social, cultural, economic, political and religious system in Korea. Even within Christian circles, opposition to the equality of women has two distinct roots: cultural patterns which place men over women, and a biblical fallacy. Until these conditions change, discrimination against women will continue in Korea."[27]

Asian nations can be authoritarian and patriarchal: their policies are slanted to make it easier for males. Consequently, modern Asian women are becoming activists and establishing women's organizations; they want to experience non-Western forms of modernity and women's movements. However, this does not mean Asian women are empowered.[28] In 1993 Prime Minister Goh Chok Tong openly endorsed gender equality through the modern Singapore government's position on patriarchy, resulting in some improvements in gender equity; nevertheless, the uphill battle against patriarchy continues in this city nation.[29] Just across the borders of Singapore, modern Malaysian women share in their nation's development as participants in the workforce and as students in universities and yet they continue to experience disadvantage: discriminatory laws and neglect (especially rural women); and they face the stresses of juggling work and family life (urban women).[30]

Being Women in the Asian 10/40 Window

Close to 49.6 percent of the world's population – about 3.6 billion – is female.[31] As cited above, at least 2.2 billion women are Asian.[32] Most of these women

---

25. Roces and Edwards, 10–12.

26. Hnuni, "Contextualizing Asian Theologies," 138.

27. Rebekah Sangwha Kim Moon, "Women, Culture and Religion: A Korean Perspective," in *Culture, Women and Theology*, ed. John S. Pobee (New Delhi: ISPCK, 1994); cited in Hnuni.

28. Roces and Edwards, "Contesting Gender Narratives," 14–15.

29. Chan, "Status of Women," 39–58.

30. Stivens, "Becoming Modern," 16–28.

31. The World Bank, "Population, Female (% of Total)."

32. United Nations Population Division, "WPP2015 POP."

live in the area known as the 10/40 window where poverty is rampant and Muslims or Communists (e.g. in China) outnumber Christians. Here, women are not as free as men to enjoy basic human rights; neither are they able to have access to education as most families cannot afford to send their daughters to school. Families prefer to send their daughters to work in the fields or streets, or marry them off in exchange for gifts.

According to the Joshua Project,[33] the 10/40 window (the term was coined by evangelist Luis Bush) comprises nations within "The Resistant Belt" and includes "the majority of the world's Muslims, Hindus, and Buddhists."[34] A significant proportion of Asian women in the 10/40 window live in Muslim nations where women are treated as low-class beings. Many of these nations are opposed to the gospel. Map 1 shows Asian nations that restrict or remain hostile to the gospel.

Map 1: Muslims in the 10/40 Window: Asia [and Africa] (Global Mapping International, cited in Joshua Project)

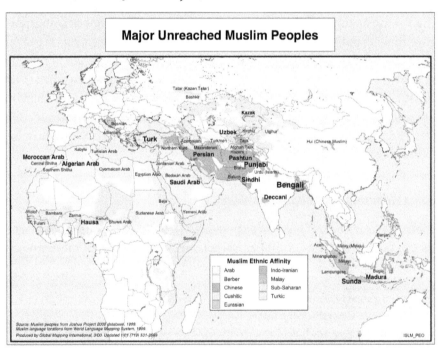

33. Information about the Joshua Project can be found at http://www.joshuaproject.net/ joshua-project.php. Essentially, it is a "research initiative" that identifies ethnic people groups, provides updates on unreached people groups and provides data to churches and Christian movements involved in establishing new churches.

34. Joshua Project, "What Is the 10/40 Window?"

The question that arises relates to an Asian Christian woman's place in patriarchal and religiously restricted nations: how do culture and religion influence leadership opportunities for Asian women in Christian ministries in these nations?

A Selection of Asian Sayings Regarding Women

Selected Asian sayings about women provide insights into the religious and cultural environment that nurtures and influences Asian Christian women servant-leaders. Asian women are viewed not through rose-tinted spectacles but through the traditional lens of proverbial sayings passed down from generation to generation. The following sayings highlight briefly the three main influences – Confucianism, Hinduism and Islam – that are representative of the religious backgrounds of the ten Asian Christian women servant-leaders whose narratives are given in this book.

Women and Confucianism

The Confucian philosophy has a tremendous influence in Asia. Mainly adopted by the Chinese people, this philosophy has also permeated nations such as South Korea, Indonesia, Malaysia, Singapore and Vietnam.

Confucianism teaches that women have no dignity or basic rights. A woman owes obedience to her father, and then to her husband upon marriage; when women become widows, they must be obedient to their sons. In fact, in Confucianism, women are to submit themselves to all men.[35] Rosenlee observes that women who embrace Confucianism and accept their roles as wife and mother are socially recognized and accepted within the Chinese family or community; unmarried women are not accepted and have no dignity – they are regarded as a humiliation in Chinese society.[36]

The biography of the mother of Chinese philosopher Mencius, in *Biographies of Admirable Women*, states that

> A woman's duties are to cook the five grains, heat the wine, look after her parents-in-law, make clothes, and that is all!
>
> A woman's duty is not to control or take charge.[37]

---

35. Ebry, *Chinese Civilization*, 253.
36. Rosenlee, *Confucianism and Women*, 127.
37. Quoted at "Confucian Inspired Sayings," para. 1.

In the same text, Madam Ban Zhao, a female Confucian philosopher and historian, observes:

Let a woman modestly yield to others; let her respect others; let her put others first, herself, last.

Lay the (girl) baby (at birth) below the bed to plainly indicate that she is lowly and weak, and should regard it as her primary duty to humble herself before others.[38]

Confucianism may possibly mean "different things to different thinkers and intellectuals," and in the past, women would have acceded to the system and philosophy in order to live peacefully.[39] In a society that demeans women, women's compliance with these expectations is a reality.

Women and Hinduism

The Hindu scriptures suggest that women and men share the same spiritual nature and prescribe the same pathway to a fulfilled life. This does not, however, translate into equal status or opportunity for women and men in Hindu society.

The majority of the population in India do not welcome a baby girl due to the practice of providing a dowry to the husband's family at her marriage. In the city of Andhra Pradesh, due to economic pressures and the chore of bringing up baby girls, there is a saying that "educating a girl is like manuring a neighbor's courtyard," because a baby girl is not raised, educated and nurtured for her own family's benefit but for another family's benefit.[40] Although giving a dowry has been illegal since 1961, the practice continues; a girl's family often feel the pressure to give a good dowry when their daughter marries.[41] A dowry can be money or gifts given "in kind," such as a house, car or furnishings. There are still reports of new daughters-in-law being mistreated (often burned) because their family only provided a small dowry;[42] Shingh also confirms that brides whose families are not able to pay the requested dowry to the groom and his family are victimized and sometimes murdered.[43]

Mohandas Gandhi, known as the Father of India, had a positive view of women. He was an advocate for independence, freedom and nonviolence.

---

38. Quoted at "Confucian Inspired Sayings," para. 3.
39. Kim and Pettid, *Women and Confucianism*, 3, 6.
40. Hnuni, "Contextualizing Asian Theologies," 141.
41. "The Dowry Prohibition Act, 1961."
42. Hnuni, "Contextualizing Asian Theologies," 141.
43. Shingh, "Dowry System," para. 6.

After he became the leader of the Indian National Congress in 1921, he worked towards demolishing poverty, expanding women's rights and ending untouchability.[44] Gandhi made the following statements about women:

> Woman is more fitted than man to make exploration and take bolder action in nonviolence.

> There is no occasion for women to consider themselves subordinate or inferior to men.

> Woman is the companion of man, gifted with equal mental capacity.

> If by strength is meant moral power, then woman is immeasurably man's superior.

> If nonviolence is the law of our being, the future is with women.[45]

A report of six men who brutally gang-raped, stripped and threw a young girl out of a moving bus demonstrates the contradictions between the philosophy of Gandhi and the reality of how women are treated in current-day India. Sonia Gandhi, the chief of India's governing party, vowed to "battle the pervasive, the shameful social attitudes and mindset that allow men to rape and molest girls with such an impunity."[46] Gandhi's philosophy and the reality of how women are treated in twenty-first-century India stand in sharp contrast.

Women and Islam

In religious practices, Muslim women do not enjoy as much favor as men. The prophet Mohammed said, "Prayer is annulled by a dog, a donkey and women (if they pass in front of the praying people)."[47]

The following verse in The Noble Qur'an explicitly allows men to abuse women:

> Men are in charge of women by [right of] what Allah has given one over the other and what they spend [for maintenance] from their wealth. So righteous women are devoutly obedient, guarding in [the husband's] absence what Allah would have them guard. But those [wives] from whom you fear arrogance – [first] advise them; [then if they persist], forsake them in bed; and [finally],

---

44. Untouchability is related to the lowest caste in India's caste system: members of higher castes consider people in the lowest caste impure and less human, and therefore untouchable.

45. Moore, "Quotes," para. 7.

46. Associated Press, "Body of a Woman," para. 13.

47. *Hadith of Bukhari*, Vol. 1, Book 9, No. 490; in Pickthall, *The Meaning*.

strike them. But if they obey you [once more], seek no means against them. (Surat An-Nisa 4:34)

Professor Leila Ahmed argues that Sura 33:35 declares "the absolute moral and spiritual equality of men and women:"[48]

For Muslim men and women,
For believing men and women,
For devout men and women,
For true (truthful) men and women,
For men and women who are
Patient and constant, for men
And women who humble themselves,
For men and women who give
In charity, for men and women
Who fast (and deny themselves),
For men and women who
Guard their chastity, and
For men and women who
Engage much in God's praise,
For them has God prepared
Forgiveness and a great reward. (Sura 33:35)

There seems to be a contradiction within Islamic beliefs, and Asian Christian men and women from Muslim backgrounds or cultures face this additional challenge regarding perspectives relating to women and women in leadership.

Summary

Socio-cultural factors tend to influence Asian Christian women servant-leaders' journeys into leadership, even within Christian communities. The influence of culture and faith backgrounds may also affect the way Asian Christian women perceive themselves and their abilities, their desire to be educated and their aspirations to become leaders. These influences increase when religious traditions are practiced in homes, in schools, in workplaces and in every form of intercultural activity. Asian Christian women servant-

---

48. Ahmed, *Women and Gender*, 64–65.

leaders continue to reveal the ethnic and cultural influences in their lives in their narratives.

Asian society is also heavily influenced by diverse factors: Confucianism, Hinduism and Islam; shamanism and postmodernism. As women's subservience within family and marriage relationships, and in society, is guided by a complex patriarchal cultural and religious context, it is probable that patriarchal ideas will then influence Christian communities. Women who desire to obey God by serving as servant-leaders in churches and mission fields, or even choose to work in an office environment in senior roles, may encounter challenges to these aspirations.

3

Understanding
Asian Evangelical
Christian Servant-Leaders

In the Asian context, the religions of Hinduism, Buddhism and Islam also offer various understandings of salvation and eternal life to their believers. Briefly, in monotheistic religions – such as Judaism, Islam and Christianity – the offer of salvation and eternal life is related to the removal of the moral barrier of sin so that humans can be restored to God.[1] In contrast, the pantheistic religions – such as Hinduism and New Age practices – believe that "self is the ultimate reality and therefore humanity's problem is epistemological."[2] Eastern religions – such as Buddhism and Taoism – think of salvation as an illumination of oneself and being able to conform "to the eternal law that governs existence."[3] As they seek to live their authentic life in Jesus in Asian contexts, Christians need to contend with the presence of various religious interpretations of life that are often culturally dominant and deeply embedded in society.

An evangelical understanding of what it might mean to be Christian in an Asian context, as well as a discussion on biblical leadership qualities, is presented in this chapter. Pandita Ramabai, a twentieth-century convert from Hinduism, modeled the passion of an Asian Christian servant-leader in the kingdom of God.

---

1. Valea, "Salvation," para. 3.
2. Valea, para. 3.
3. Valea, para. 3.

An Evangelical Understanding of Being a Christian

An evangelical[4] understanding of Christian leadership is based on the evangelical doctrines of salvation (faith encounters) and service (ministry). In this book, Christian leadership in Asia is viewed from an evangelical theological perspective.

There are three key terms in the language of salvation: justification, sanctification and glorification.[5]

In the ten narratives that you will read later, six Asian Christian women servant-leaders revealed that initially they struggled to understand the evangelical concept of salvation.

Salvation

Evangelical Christians believe that the first step to Christian obedience involves the confession that Jesus Christ is Lord and a belief in the heart that Jesus died for human sin and has been raised from the dead by God. Consequently, the believer experiences an assurance that shame and condemnation have been replaced by honor and salvation: "because, if you confess with your mouth that Jesus is Lord and believe in your heart that God raised him from the dead, you will be saved. For with the heart one believes and is justified, and with the mouth one confesses and is saved. For the Scripture says, 'Everyone who believes in him will not be put to shame'" (Rom 10:9–11).

Justification

Ryrie notes that this faith confession in Christ results in the new Christian being declared righteous or justified. This new Christian has been reconciled with God. Justification by faith in Christ delivers us from sin and therefore our lives are marked as holy or sanctified. As Ryrie puts it, "unproductive faith is not genuine faith; therefore, what we are in Christ will be seen in what we become before men [sic] . . . justification assures us of peace in God (Rom 5:1)."[6]

---

4. According to the *New Oxford American Dictionary*, the adjective "evangelical" means "according to the teaching of the gospel or the Christian religion," "denoting a tradition within Protestant Christianity emphasizing the authority of the Bible, personal conversion, and the doctrine of salvation by faith in the Atonement" or "zealous in advocating something." The noun "evangelical" refers to "a member of the evangelical tradition in the Christian church."

5. Chan, *Spiritual Theology*, 84.

6. Ryrie, *Basic Theology*, 343–345.

The apostle Paul reminds us that true Christian salvation does not allow for any additions to the gospel: "yet we know that a person is not justified by works of the law but through faith in Jesus Christ, so we also have believed in Christ Jesus, in order to be justified by faith in Christ and not by works of the law, because by works of the law no one will be justified" (Gal 2:16).

Therefore, intimacy with God the Father through Christ, the Son, and experienced by the Christian, is the salvation born out of the working of grace by the Holy Spirit.[7]

Sanctification

Ryrie indicates that sanctification refers to a believer becoming progressively more holy when personal faith is placed in Jesus Christ. Ultimate sanctification will be attained in heaven when we will be "completely and eternally set apart to our God (Eph 5:26–27; Jude 24–25). The work of the Holy Spirit is prominent during this process":[8] "It is by the Spirit that we put to death the deeds of the body (Rom 8:13). The Spirit ignites love in our hearts (Rom 5:5). By the Spirit we are changed from glory to glory to become more and more like Jesus (2 Cor 3:18). And it is the fruit of the Spirit that produces in us Christlikeness, which is the goal of sanctification (Gal 5:22–23)."[9]

Chan reminds us that sanctification is not representative of a more advanced phase than justification but is a continuous process of transformation into Christlikeness.[10]

Glorification

Various traditional theologies view glorification – also known as perfection – as growth in Christian life that "see[s] its completion in the consummation beyond history" because sinless perfection is not attainable this side of eternity.[11]

The apostle Paul refers to the state of glorification that is an act of God in Romans 8:30: "And those whom he predestined he also called, and those whom he called he also justified, and those whom he justified he also glorified" (Rom 8:30).

---

7. Chan, *Spiritual Theology*, 87.
8. Ryrie, *Basic Theology*, 442–443.
9. Ryrie, 443.
10. Chan, *Spiritual Theology*, 88–89.
11. Chan, 97.

The soteriological and eschatological intent is evident in that God purposed "to bring his human creation back into a fullness of relation with himself, owned by him and sustained by him and given to share in his splendor."[12] Glorification then becomes a final and complete transformation to Christ's image, made possible only through the "eschatological Adam, the risen Christ who in his resurrection was crowned with glory and honor and given dominion over all things" (see Ps 8:4–6 and 1 Cor 15:20–27).[13]

In other words, glorification is a privileged state of blessedness in which Christian believers express God's glory and power in their lives. It is first made possible by the initial salvation process of believing in and conforming to Christ, and continues into the "hope of sharing his [Christ's] risen life"[14] through current life circumstances and into the "heavenly condition and dignity."[15] Cranfield states that conformity to Christ's image and the final glorification are intended in the expression in Romans 8:30.[16] The tension of experiencing the glory of Christ through daily obedience, sufferings and victories exists with the future hope of final glorification.[17]

Service

The Spirit-led progression into Christlikeness, together with the adoption of biblical disciplines to sustain a holy lifestyle, will inevitably lead the saints to serve God. The apostle Paul reminds us: "Therefore, if anyone is in Christ, he is a new creation. The old has passed away; behold, the new has come. All this is from God, who through Christ reconciled us to himself and gave us the ministry of reconciliation; that is, in Christ God was reconciling the world to himself, not counting their trespasses against them, and entrusting to us the message of reconciliation. Therefore, we are ambassadors for Christ" (2 Cor 5:17–20a).

As followers of Jesus Christ we have been entrusted with the message of reconciliation so that we can continue the ministry of reconciliation. Believers who perform this service are designated ambassadors of Christ. Performing this role links believers to the "Great Commission": going and making disciples

---

12. Dunn, *Romans 1–8*, 495.
13. Dunn, 495.
14. Dunn, 495.
15. Unger, *New Unger's Bible Dictionary*, 479.
16. Cranfield, *Epistle to the Romans*, 432.
17. Cranfield, 433.

of all nations, baptizing and teaching others to obey God under the authority that is given by Jesus (Matt 28:18–20).

Evangelical Theology in the Asian Context

"The designation *evangelical* arises from the Greek term *evangelion* which means gospel in English."[18] Evangelical Christians believe and devote themselves to the gospel message of Jesus Christ, maintain and trust the Bible as the source of their beliefs, and experience the Word in their life and deeds.[19]

Evangelical theology in Asia needs to be contextual: "relevance to our context is imperative."[20] In the Seoul Declaration, members of the Asia Theological Association (ATA) consultation – comprising evangelicals from Asia, Africa and Latin America – while recognizing its contribution, criticized Western theology as being "largely rationalistic, molded by Western philosophies and preoccupied with intellectual concerns."[21]

Evangelical theology in Asia is contextualized theology: the Word remains relevant to the cultures[22] because in Asia, theology must consider issues of poverty, hunger, war, demon possession, bribery, cheating, idolatry, the resurgence of Asian religions and Communism.[23]

While Asian evangelical theology seems largely to be in agreement with Western theology over basic beliefs, such as the authority of the Bible, the Trinity, the incarnation of Jesus Christ, the concept of sin and redemption, and the ministry of making Christ known, there seems to be a strong suggestion that Asian people from a variety of religious and social backgrounds are beginning to re-interpret the Bible from their perspectives.[24]

For example, Asia is a hotbed of religious pluralism. Asian society is entrenched with a mixture of religions, cultures and ethnicities. Western evangelists arrived in Asia and taught that Christianity was superior to any other religions (I was a recipient of such a notion at a young age). Asians rejected this notion as a form of extreme arrogance. Indigenous Asian evangelicals living among ethnic, tribal and religious groups wanted to keep

---

18. Grenz, *Revisioning Evangelical Theology*, 22.
19. Grenz, 34–35.
20. Gnanakan, *Biblical Theology*, iii.
21. Gnanakan, 280.
22. Athyal, "Asian Christian Theology," 50, 52.
23. Ro, "Contextualization," 73.
24. Tano, "Toward an Evangelical Theology," 99.

the harmony between the various groups of people while humbly seeking to inform and explain the supremacy of Christ.

Therefore, building bridges with a person from another faith group is crucial in our endeavor to make Christ known. Instead of "shoving" Christ to the people, we begin to "share" Christ's love and grace in the hope that those who hear will be drawn to Christ, and will discover and recognize his supremacy. Growing up in Singapore, which is multicultural, multiracial and multilingual, I remember hating any professing Christian trying to push the gospel message with verbal aggression.

In the Asian context, the issue of respecting and not shaming another person's belief system because of religious or racial difference matters. When my Hindu grandfather passed away, I was still in Bible college. As the eldest granddaughter, it was expected of me to offer my grandfather due respect at the Hindu funeral. As I had had the satisfaction of caring for my grandfather in small ways while he was alive, it did not bother me at all when my parents quietly advised that I could be present at the funeral but it would be better for me to leave before the Hindu rites began so that my non-participation would not give rise to questions among the Hindu crowd. I respected my parents and my grandfather enough to understand this suggestion – it would be shameful for the family if I had stayed on. However, I was also thankful that my parents acknowledged that I should pay my last respects to my grandfather before the Hindu rites began – this was honoring to my parents. The value of honoring our parents is extremely important in Asia and it is also biblical. Christians in Asia often live in this cultural and religious tension. And these are the tensions that influence evangelical servant-leaders, both men and women, as they serve the Lord Jesus Christ.

Biblical Servant-Leadership

In the Asian Christian community, the definition and boundaries given to biblical leadership either limit or release gifted Asian Christian women to step into their calling. The characteristics or qualities of biblical leadership are many and may be exhibited by Christians regardless of whether they are in leadership roles or not. Those who are called to leadership roles, however, must demonstrate a loosely bounded set of these qualities if they are to have an effective and sustained ministry. Some of the key qualities that have been studied and expected of Christian servant-leaders are humility,[25] love,[26] intimacy with God,[27] faith in God,[28] acceptance of diversity,[29] pursuit of unity,[30] stewardship[31] and truthfulness.[32] The sanctification of the Christian servant-leader by the power of the Holy Spirit inevitably leads to the demonstration of the power of the gospel in both conduct and service in the kingdom of God.

Pandita Ramabai, referred to later in this chapter, is an example of that unique power of the gospel in a twentieth-century Asian Christian woman servant-leader.

Christian leaders are expected to be visionary influencers,[33] have passion and commitment, and to be risk-takers. Biblical leadership is servant-leadership.[34] Jesus exemplified servant-leadership with authority and humility (John 13:3–15). He taught his disciples not to abuse their authority as leaders (Matt 20:25–26), but to have an attitude of sacrificial service (Matt 20:27–28). The servant-leader is not exempt from suffering (Isa 53:12–17) and is exhorted to remain in God's love so that others may receive God's love through the leader's ministry (John 15:9–17).

J. Robert Clinton studied biblical leadership and concluded that Christian leaders demonstrate a "God-given capacity and God-given responsibility to influence a specific group of people toward God's purposes for the group."[35] The

---

25. Humility is a quality that touches God's heart. He expects it of us and he showed us the way; see Prov 3:33–35; 22:4; Matt 5:5; 18:3–4; 23:12; Phil 1:2–11; 1 Pet 5:6–7.

26. Love is the foundation of all that Christians are and do. God expects us to love him and our neighbors, and he showed the way; see Deut 7:9; Prov 8:17; Jer 31:3; John 13:34–35; 14:15; 1 John 4:10–11.

27. Intimacy with God is an innate desire, a longing, to know God; see Pss 42:1–2; 63:1–11; Luke 6:12; Phil 3:7–10; Col 3:1; Jas 4:8a.

28. Faith in God is an essential first step – both saving faith and living faith are needed to carry out God's plans. God's gifts of wisdom and grace are related to this faith; see 2 Cor 5:7; Eph 2:8–10; 3:17–19; Heb 11:16; Jas 1:5–8.

29. Acceptance of diversity was modeled by Jesus when he recruited a team made up of diverse personalities and equipped and launched them into God's Great Commission; see Matt 4:18–22; 28:19–20; Rom 15:7; 1 Cor 12:12–30; Col 3:11; Rev 7:9–10.

30. Unity was the theme of Jesus's prayer in John 17. God is a pursuer of unity; see Eccl 4:9–10; Ps 133:1; Eph 4:1–6, 11–13; John 17:21.

31. Stewardship is a responsible exercise of sharing God-given gifts, whether it be time, efforts, money, talents or any other possessions; see Deut 8:18; Prov 3:27–28; Matt 25:14–30; Luke 16:1–13; 1 Cor 4:2; 1 Tim 6:17–18.

32. Truthfulness is closely related to integrity. God desires his leaders to be honest, upright and reliable in word and deeds; see Exod 20:16; Prov 11:3; 16:11; Luke 16:10; Rom 12:3.

33. Haggai, *Influential Leader*, 17–21.

34. Wilkes, *Jesus on Leadership*; Hunt and Hutcheson, *Leadership for Women*.

35. Clinton, *The Making*, 202.

leader's main task must be the influential direction toward God's purposes.[36] Challenges remain for the individual called into leadership. This is where the leader "personally must be what God wants him or her to be . . . be involved in raising up other leaders . . . be in tune with God's purposes for them."[37] In addition, Clinton states that leadership "evolves and emerges over a lifetime . . . a lifetime of God's lessons."[38]

According to George Barna, leadership is not synonymous with influence – influence is a product of great leadership. Leadership is not management but a directional thrust towards effectiveness; it is not about gaining control or power but empowering others into leadership; it is not about popularity but a readiness to pursue the vision.[39]

Biblical Servant-Leadership Qualities

Aubrey Malphurs references his book *Building Leaders* (2004) in his online article discussing both the definition of leadership and the characteristics of biblical leadership. Malphurs agrees with the authors mentioned above that "Christian leaders are servants."[40] Christian leaders are godly and must have direction, a vision and a mission.[41] Malphurs adds that "leaders have followers . . . If a person has no followers, he is not a leader."[42]

Humility and Love as Marks of the Effective Servant-Leader

According to the Scriptures, leadership always aligns with servanthood. *Diakonia*[43] – service or ministry – is the Greek word most often used in the New Testament.

---

36. Clinton, 203.
37. Clinton, 205.
38. Clinton, 205.
39. Barna, *Fish Out of Water*, 3–7.
40. Malphurs, "Growing Leaders," para. 2.
41. Malphurs, paras. 3–4.
42. Malphurs, para. 5.
43. The Greek word *diakonia* (G1248) reflects the ministerial heart of the servant. According to Greek Concordance online (http://biblehub.com/greek/1249.htm), this word defines someone who executes the command of a master. The executor of services is known as servant, minister or attendant. This person could be the servant of a king, a deacon of the church or a waiter serving at a table. Unger expresses specifically that "*Diakonos* [G1249] is usually employed in relation to the ministry of the gospel" (Unger, *New Unger's Bible Dictionary*, 872).

Mark 10:45 and parallels are foundational:

> For even the Son of Man came not to be served but to serve, and to give his life as a ransom for many. (Mark 10:45)

> [Because God] has made us competent to be ministers [*diakonoi*] of a new covenant, not of the letter but of the Spirit. For the letter kills, but the Spirit gives life. (2 Cor 3:6)

> Just as you learned it from Epaphras our beloved fellow servant [*diakonia*]. He is a faithful minister [*diakonos*] of Christ on your behalf. (Col 1:7)

> As for you, always be sober-minded, endure suffering, do the work of an evangelist, fulfill your ministry [*diakonia*]. (2 Tim 4:5)

For Robert Greenleaf, the term "servant-leader" conjures up a particular image – the servant-leader is a servant before becoming a leader.[44] Making the choice to serve "brings one to aspire to lead."[45] Greenleaf relates servant-leadership to the state of those being served; he asks, "do they, *while being served*, become healthier, wiser, freer, more autonomous, more likely themselves to become servants?"[46]

Wilkes, in his book *Jesus on Leadership*, outlines seven principles of leadership modeled after our Lord Jesus Christ. These principles demonstrate a strong thread of humility. Christian leaders are expected to (1) be humble and allow God to exalt them; (2) obey God and not seek positions; (3) be a servant and find greatness in service; (4) be a risk-taker by serving others; (5) be responsible to, and (6) be accountable to, authority; (7) be a builder of a team. Leaders are not successful unless they empower others to step into their shoes.

Clinton's three challenges resonate with the need for leaders to remain humble: Christian ministry leaders must desire to be all that they can be according to God's plans; they must be aware of emerging leaders; and they must partner with God in the selection process of future leaders.[47]

According to Greenleaf, a Christian leader who exercises humility realizes that

---

44. Greenleaf, *Servant as Leader*, 15.
45. Greenleaf, 15.
46. Greenleaf, 15.
47. Clinton, *The Making*, 196–197.

... caring for persons, the more able and the less able serving each other, is the rock upon which a good society is built ... If a better society is to be built, one that is more just and loving, one that provides greater creative opportunity for its people, then the most open course is to raise both the capacity to serve and the very performance as servant of existing major institutions by new regenerative forces operating within them.[48]

The Lord Jesus Christ exemplified this image of servant-leadership. He was a spiritual leader and ministered as a teacher, preacher and healer (Luke 4:18). He had authority and had an intimate knowledge of God. In an exhibition of profound humility born out of love for his disciples, he washed their feet (John 13:4–5). He built a deep intimacy with his Father in heaven – he stayed awake through the early hours before dawn in prayerful communion (Mark 1:35). In that same humility, Jesus recruited and accepted a team of twelve disciples from diverse backgrounds and personalities: they brought their differences to the table of fellowship (see the Gospels). Jesus modeled a responsible stewardship: he embraced his calling to the point of death (Phil 2:5–11). He loved the disciples to the end (John 13:1).

Jesus said to his disciples that "If anyone would be first, he must be last of all and servant of all" (Mark 9:35), referring to the selfless nature expected of leaders who worship God.

Intimacy with God and Faith in God as Marks of the Visionary Servant-Leader

Haggai reminds visionary leaders to yield to the Lordship of Christ[49] and discipline self to a "conscious dependence on God."[50]

Intimacy with God is translated into a theology of leadership where we build good-quality relationships, respect the diversity of followers' gifts, are responsible for a transparent lifestyle within and outside of the work, and establish and fulfill covenantal relationships. Covenantal relationships that "induce freedom, not paralysis are promoted. A covenantal relationship rests on shared commitment to ideas ... open to influence."[51] In the covenantal

---

48. Greenleaf, *Institution as Servant*, 9.
49. Haggai, *Influential Leader*, 97.
50. Haggai, *Influential Leader*, 111.
51. De Pree, *Leadership*, 60.

relationship, leaders have the possibility to take risks with unusual people with unusual ideas.[52]

The Christian leader's intimacy with God is closely related to the leader's prayerfulness. Prayerfulness is the transparent demonstration of faith in God. Consistently the New Testament emphasizes that nothing can be achieved apart from communion with God. Jesus underlines this for the first disciples and for us: "I am the vine; you are the branches. Whoever abides in me and I in him, he it is that bears much fruit, for apart from me you can do nothing" (John 15:5). This connects to another crucial reason for prayer – that the Holy Spirit would fill them through concentrated, fervent and sanctified prayer (Acts 1:8; 4:31; Rom 8:27). Though it is possible to be a secular leader without the Holy Spirit's intervention and activity, it is crucial for a Christian leader to yield to the power of God's Spirit. During prayer, God rewards his people with wisdom that is necessary to encounter challenges and accomplish his purposes. The apostle Paul exhorts believers to bring all their anxieties to God, in prayer and with a thankful heart. An exchange of anxieties for peace that passes all understanding is a worthwhile option for servant-leaders (Phil 4:6–7). Finally, prayerful leaders will discover God's agenda for themselves and their ministries. Jesus demonstrated a prayerful attitude toward his ministry. Mark 1:30–39 and other passages in the Gospels reveal that Jesus had regular communion with his Father.[53]

Leaders who are intimate with God are persons of faith who have been able to influence their generation and others. They are people who have seen and experienced more than others. Visionary leaders have foresight and insight: they see hope in difficult situations and are willing to step ahead while taking calculated risks.[54]

Greenleaf describes foresight as the "lead" that enables leaders to move ahead. Once they lose this foresight, leaders cease to make decisions that are aligned to their vision. This ultimately causes leaders to react to immediate situations rather than to respond with solutions that will propel followers ahead in line with their vision. An insightful leader is someone who lives within a

---

52. De Pree, 60. De Pree further explains that leaders are obliged to think about building and nurturing intimacy that subsequently will be reflected in leaders' work ethics and in the way personal or corporate values are incorporated into these work ethics. He challenges leaders to have an intimate knowledge of their work and of people with whom they work. He exhorts leaders to discover the visions of those working with them (58–61).

53. Blackaby and Blackaby, *Spiritual Leadership*, 183–185.

54. Sanders, *Spiritual Leadership*, 55–57.

unity of the past, present and future – and continues to move ahead. "Living this way is partly a matter of faith."[55]

Christian leaders' deep fellowship and prayerful communion with God, the Creator of the heavens and earth, will fill their lives with reverence. Christian leaders' complete dependence on God's Spirit sets them apart and allows them to recognize, with the apostle Paul, the grace of God that offers the sufficiency and competency to be faithful ministers despite an onslaught of trials, sufferings or persecutions: "[This is] the confidence that we have through Christ toward God. Not that we are sufficient in ourselves to claim anything as coming from us, but our sufficiency is from God, who has made us competent to be ministers of a new covenant, not of the letter but of the Spirit" (2 Cor 3:4–6).

Though Christian leaders have a mandate to be visionaries, their visions from God are a consequence of their personal intimacy with God. Intimacy with God through spiritual disciplines, such as prayer and studying the Word of God, release leaders into this mandate. Leaders do not work alone – they need a team to carry out this vision.

Acceptance of Diversity as a Mark of the Servant-Leader

Our Lord Jesus exemplified the acceptance of diversity when he called Jews from various backgrounds, professions and temperaments into his team. His ministry team included fishermen, tax collectors and one who would betray him. He called mild-mannered, quickly discouraged and impulsive disciples. The Lord loved his betrayer, Judas Iscariot, and the rest of this mixed crew to the end (John 13:1): a sign of acceptance born out of godly love.

Leaders need to accept the diversity of people from different walks of life so that the variety of gifts brought in by different people may be harnessed for the progress of the institution.[56] Leaders also have a responsibility to create a dynamic culture within the leadership team. While this sounds like a serious risk to take, leaders who are dependent on God will recognize, maximize and reward the differences and be the leading force in team synergy.[57]

Diversity does have its challenges. In an article that recognizes the multicultural diversity in globally minded companies, Kelley Holland poses the challenge and its solution that applies to multicultural and multinational

---

55. Greenleaf, *Servant as Leader*, 26–27.
56. De Pree, *Leadership*, 10.
57. Blackaby and Blackaby, *Spiritual Leadership*, 298–302.

congregations in churches pursuing God's Great Commission: "A gorgeous mosaic? You bet. But multicultural teams can also be tricky to manage. Communications style can differ from culture to culture, as can traditional views of hierarchy and decision-making processes – and of course, there can be language barriers. The potential for misunderstanding, bungled efforts and ill-will is enormous. The key to success is understanding and accepting the differences in a multicultural team, and then using them to enhance the way the team analyzes situations and makes decisions."[58]

The Bible provides many illustrations of diversity: racial (Jew and Gentiles), social status (slave or free) and gender (men and women). God's solution for such diversity and the possible tensions is: "you are all one in Christ Jesus" (Gal 3:28).

Pursuit of Unity as a Mark of the Servant-Leader

The apostle Paul reminds and exhorts believers to understand that, though we may be many members, as Christians we are the body of Christ, and therefore we all belong to each other (Rom 12:5; 1 Cor 6:15; 10:17; 12:20, 27).

Psalm 133:1 states, "Behold, how good and pleasant it is when brothers dwell in unity!" The Lord Jesus prayed for unity (John 17) for his disciples because he recognized they needed to keep their faith during the tumultuous times of those days. The apostle Peter wrote his exhortation "Finally, all of you, have unity of mind, sympathy, brotherly love, a tender heart, and a humble mind" (1 Pet 3:8) to a group of people suffering persecution. Unity was then, and still is, important for a team's growth in faith during difficult or good times. Every believer can be a "channel of unity" and be the "scent of life" to non-Christians: "The sight of loving unity among believers arrests the unbeliever."[59]

The Christian Conference of Asia (CCA), in their online document "Mission in Unity and Contextual Theology," emphasize the churches' calling to participate in the mission of God and witness to Christ in unity. The gospel's power, best exhibited in the unity of the body of Christ, becomes an empowering force in the mission of God.[60]

The servant-leader pursues unity within his or her circle of influence to demonstrate the answer to the prayer of Jesus (John 17). As the pursuit of unity

---

58. Holland, "How Diversity Makes a Team Click," paras. 7–8.
59. White, *The Fight*, 150.
60. Christian Conference of Asia, "Mission in Unity," para. 1.

becomes a lifestyle, it will inevitably overflow to other groups, but never at the expense of gospel truths.

Even in Christian churches or organizations, imperfect people will encounter challenges to certain concepts, decisions or actions. I remember disagreeing with some decisions made by my former spiritual authority. I would normally express clearly that I disagreed with the decisions for various reasons while, at the same time, accepting the decisions for the sake of team and corporate unity. At times, it would be my former spiritual authority who disagreed with me, but he would accept my decision over my areas of responsibility. Thankfully, these were rare moments.

Stewardship and Trustworthiness as Marks of the Excellent Servant-Leader

Evangelical servant-leaders understand that nothing belongs to them – not time, money, materials or relationships; God owns everything. "You shall remember the LORD your God, for it is he who gives you power to get wealth, that he may confirm his covenant that he swore to your fathers, as it is this day" (Deut 8:18).

Leaders need to think of themselves as stewards, not owners. Leaders possess the privilege of making a difference in the lives of their followers while enjoying "the special privileges of complexity, of ambiguity, of diversity."[61]

Greenleaf uses the term "trustees" in reference to the governing body of an institution, that is, the leadership. Trustees must have the trust of their people which is a direct result of their responsibility to care enough about every aspect of the organization, exercising their administrative and visionary possibilities to make the impossible possible.[62]

Accepting imperfect people requires tolerance, according to Greenleaf. Anyone can lead perfect people – but since there are no such people, leaders need empathy to lead imperfect people.[63] Imperfect people must be "accepted for what they are, even though their performance may be judged critically in terms of what they are capable of doing."[64] When leaders empathize with their followers and journey alongside them, there is a greater likelihood that their followers will trust them.[65]

---

61. De Pree, *Leadership*, 22–23.
62. Greenleaf, *Institution as Servant*, 7–10.
63. Greenleaf, *Servant as Leader*, 22.
64. Greenleaf, 23.
65. Greenleaf, 23.

The diligent stewardship of relationships, talents, ideas and ministries that God entrusts to us can only be carried out when we empty ourselves of the notions that we are the owners of all those assets. Our stewardship is best carried out clothed in humility, and, as we persevere in this responsibility, others will begin to trust us as they see God trusts us.

Pandita Ramabai: Woman of the Millennium

The Gospel narratives teach that Jesus exemplified humility born out of love for God and people. James 4:6 emphasizes that God gives grace to the humble and opposes the proud. Pandita Ramabai is an example of servant-leadership for our times.

A Brahmin convert to Christianity, Pandita Ramabai (1858–1922) was recognized posthumously, in 1989, by the Indian Government as the Woman of the Millennium. She was the first Indian woman to be awarded this highest honor for community service. Despite her humble beginnings, Ramabai became the first Bible translator, established ministries that catered to the needs of high-caste widows, protected the interests of women, discouraged child marriages and established a school for the visually handicapped.

An Indian woman born into the highest caste in the nineteenth century, Pandita Ramabai was a twentieth-century apostle to the Indian people, especially to children, the destitute and prostitutes. Ramabai was home-schooled in a forest by her parents and committed to memory the *Puranas*, the Vedic literature that contains a vast amount of history and, as Hindus believe, is the absolute truth. They contain every instruction for living life in order to attain an eternal relationship with the Hindu Lord Krishna.

Ramabai received a scholarship to study in the United Kingdom and was considered a poet, scholar and social reformer. Ramabai's willingness to lower herself in obedience so that Christ could be exalted in and through her servant-leadership demonstrates her attitude of humility and God's grace in her life. Her humility is reflected in the way she agreed to marry a person from a non-Brahmin caste and accepted her calling to establish the Pandita Ramabai *Mukti* Mission in 1889. The word *mukti* in Sanskrit[66] means liberation; this mission continues to provide housing, food, medical care, education and vocational training for widows, orphans and many other needy groups in the twenty-first century.

---

66. Sanskrit is one of the oldest Indo-European languages.

Pandita Ramabai was released into ministry through her intimate knowledge and experience of God in her life. She wanted to tell others about Jesus and his saving grace. After encountering Romans 5:6–10 and 1 John 4:9–10 she exclaimed in her autobiography: "How good, how indescribably good! What good news for me a woman, a woman born in India, among Brahmans who hold out no hope for me and the like of me! The Bible declares that Christ did not reserve this great salvation for a particular caste or sex."[67]

Pandita Ramabai's life is an excellent example of diversity. She was God's instrument for preparing servant-leaders. Ramabai's introduction to the gospel and mission involved a diverse group comprising Americans, British and fellow Indians from different castes. Ramabai's autobiography demonstrates that her outstanding Christian leadership was shaped and launched through diverse experiences and influences including a British missionary to India, Miss Hurford, who introduced her to the New Testament; British principal Miss Beale; Catholic nuns; the Anglican Church of England; biographies of missionaries Hudson Taylor, George Müller and John Paton; and Dean Bodley of the Woman's Medical College of Pennsylvania.[68]

Pandita Ramabai had a very strong and influential sense of stewardship in relation to the gift of salvation, her ministries and the many people entrusted to her. In her autobiography, there is an account of her mission's participation in the outpouring of the Welsh revival that extended to, and affected, India:

> The news of the revival in Wales and Khassia Hills reached *Mukti* and here too people met together in daily prayer for Revival. God faithfully answered their prayers and the revival fire swept through *Mukti*. In December 1901, twelve hundred were baptized . . . One evening when Ramabai was expounding John 8, the Holy Spirit descended with power and all the girls began to pray aloud. They experienced the power of God . . . They went to Poona where three meetings were held everyday. Europeans, Indian Christians and non-Christians, famine orphans from different orphanages and schools were greatly blessed.[69]

All Christian leaders have the responsibility to be good stewards of their time, efforts, talents and wealth. More than that, Ramabai reminds us that

---

67. Ramabai, *Autobiography*, 19–20.
68. Ramabai, 13–24.
69. Ramabai, 26.

Christian leaders are to be good stewards of the gift of salvation; in other words, they are responsible for sharing the gospel with others.

Christian leaders are also responsible for the good stewardship of Christian unity. Ramabai's pursuit of unity can best be seen in the way she pursued Jesus, and in her interactions with people in different strata of society. A story in her autobiography about her daughter Manorama reveals that Ramabai always had India and the people of India in her heart. Ramabai was given a wonderful opportunity to leave her daughter behind in England so she could enjoy a better education and lifestyle. She declined the offer, saying: "I want her to be one of us, and love our country people as one of them, not as a strange or superior being . . . I do not want her to be too proud to acknowledge that she is one of India's daughters."[70]

Summary

The good news about biblical servant-leadership is that it is available to Asian Christians – both men and women. Go ahead and shout Hallelujah!

The Christian is set apart by faith alone in Christ and accepts that Jesus is the Lord of his or her life. The very first step to a faith expression in the Lord Jesus hinges on the love of God towards us and our humble response to him. Transformation into the image of Christ aligns itself with purposeful service for God. Servant-leaders walk through their living faith expressions.

There are costs to the servant-leaders' indebtedness to God and the people entrusted to them (the servant-leaders): faithful service outweighs success; reaching personal moral potential outweighs reaching goals; vulnerability and an ability to take risks are valued; intimacy, accountability and willingness to mature are part of a lifelong learning process. The servant-leaders' covenant relationship and intimacy is best reflected in the Lord's commandment to love the Lord our God with all our heart and with all our soul and with our entire mind and strength (Mark 12:30).

---

70. Ramabai, 21.

4

The Complexities of Servant-Leadership in a Christian Environment

Clinton's Leadership Emergence Theory (LET)[1] provides a Western male perspective and Elizabeth Glanville contributes a Western female perspective to the preparation and development of Christian servant-leaders.[2] The LET discussion leads into another section[3] highlighting the Western theological perspectives of complementarian and egalitarian understandings of women in leadership. A brief introduction on feminist theology from Asian perspectives is also included in this chapter.

Preparation of Christian Leaders

God uses innate qualities, life experiences, crises, personal struggles and successes to develop leaders. Sanders states, "Spiritual leadership requires superior spiritual power, which can never be generated by the self. There is no such thing as a self-made spiritual leader. A true leader influences others spiritually."[4] The Holy Spirit helps, guides and leads the Christian leader.

---

1. Clinton, *The Making*.

2. Glanville, "Leadership Development."

3. While I recognize the complementarian, egalitarian and newer feminist perspectives regarding men and women in church and family, and particularly women in church leadership, it is not my purpose to write a theology of church leadership. Rather, the purpose of this book is to explore the experiences of Asian Christian women servant-leaders and to provide a voice for them.

4. Sanders, *Spiritual Leadership*, 28.

God also develops the leader's skills. Henry and Richard Blackaby cite the example of Moses who was educated and had great leadership skills. Unfortunately, Moses assumed that everyone else could recognize his leadership skills. This produced results that landed Moses in trouble with the Egyptians and the Israelites. Forty years later, after God had trained him to be humble, Moses learned that "every divine assignment also comes with God's equipping . . . The key was not Moses' skills but Moses' surrender."[5]

God develops the leader's skills, and expects the leader to yield his or her heart to God so that God's presence permeates the projects and God's perspectives become the periscope through which to view the use of skills and the accomplishment of assignments.

Leadership Emergence Theory

Clinton proposes that God develops leaders through the six stages of LET: sovereign foundations, inner-life growth, ministry maturing, life maturing, convergence, and afterglow or celebration.[6]

In the first stage, sovereign foundations, God's providence is active from birth through family, society and historical events. The leader simply needs to respond to God positively.[7] The development process of the emerging leader – Clinton's inner-life growth stage – includes three main checks: integrity, obedience and reception of God's truth. Integrity is foundational to the Christian leader's character. Obedience is checked throughout the life of the leader by asking the question: am I learning to recognize, understand and obey God's voice? Finally, Clinton maintains that every Christian leader must be able to receive truth from God because it develops spiritual authority, which is essential for them (Christian leaders) to exercise their spiritual influence.[8]

In the third stage, ministry maturing, emerging leaders discover their spiritual gifts and how to use them to serve God. Their leadership skills are sharpened and they move on to another phase of ministry maturity. In this stage they encounter conflicts and begin to learn about relationships and how to exercise discernment in decision-making. The emerging leaders also begin to learn about spiritual authority. Through these processes, leaders learn how

---

5. Blackaby and Blackaby, *Spiritual Leadership*, 70.
6. Clinton, *The Making*, 44–47.
7. Clinton, 44.
8. Clinton, 58–66.

to submit to God in a way that pleases God. As leaders mature, God enlarges their "perspectives of the spiritual dynamics of ministry."[9] The leaders advance to the next stage, life maturing, when they are able to discern and respond accordingly to God's will.[10]

In this fourth stage, God matures leaders though a variety of significant life experiences: illness, conflicts, changes in life situations, loss of loved ones, property or livelihood, persecution, inner struggle, seeing God's character vindicated or experiencing his special intervention. In this stage, leaders have no choice but to trust God. Through their submissive responses to God, leaders mature as confident people of God. The leaders are able to minister out of their experiences of brokenness and God's compassion, recognizing how deeply they depend on God.[11]

The fifth stage, convergence, allows for the life maturing of the previous stage to merge with ministry skills. The Holy Spirit's intervention is crucial – through this merger, the leaders' calling and ministry are clarified. During this stage, they are primed to serve more effectively. Clinton notes: "One of the striking characteristics seen in effective leaders is their drive to learn. They learn from all kinds of sources. They learn from Scripture . . . learn about their own uniqueness . . . learn to use spiritual gifts."[12]

According to Clinton, very few Christians achieve the final stage of the leadership process, which he designates "afterglow." In this stage, leaders who have been successful in accomplishing God's plan in their lives begin to enjoy the influence that they can exercise in society: among their connections and with the next generation. These leaders enjoy the freedom of not having to prove their capabilities, knowledge or skills to anyone else because they are confident and secure of their significance in Christ. Other people begin to seek them out for counsel and ministry. In this phase, there is no developmental task for the leaders. Instead, they "allow a lifetime of ministry to reflect the glory of God and to honor His faithfulness over a lifetime of development."[13]

---

9. Clinton, 110.
10. Clinton, 73–123.
11. Clinton, 153–166.
12. Clinton, 175–178.
13. Clinton, 47.

Leadership Emergence Theory for Women in Christian Leadership

Elizabeth Glanville scrutinized Clinton's LET from an American women's perspective and discovered key findings related to leadership development in time, processing marked by God's shaping activity, and response.[14]

Glanville's study analyzed data from over one hundred and thirty women and yielded results related to sovereign foundations, the first stage of the LET. Elements such as "the value of education for daughters, the encouragement or permission from parents to pursue careers traditionally reserved for males, visible models and mentors of women in leadership positions, leadership opportunities, and involvement in traditionally male youth activities" emerged as shaping factors for American Christian women leaders.[15] These factors are early signs that these women could become leaders. Women also had to deal with and overcome negative factors such as the theological environment of the church, bad experiences in dysfunctional families, abusive relationships, and their own families' lack of vision for opportunities for women to become leaders.[16]

While Glanville agreed with most of Clinton's theory, an important aspect of many women's lives needed to be included as part of leadership development: the motherhood season.[17] She acknowledges that the motherhood phase may not apply to all American women leaders, and affected American women leaders may choose to focus on internal ministry rather than external ministry commitments during this season of motherhood.[18]

Glanville's findings indicate that when women accept the motherhood season as a normal part of a woman's life, they become free to use that time period to "prepare for future ministry commitments"; it need not negate a call to ministry that they might have received earlier.[19] This "cycling in and out of ministry"[20] during the motherhood season is described as a "phenomenon among women."[21] Decisions made by these women who value relationships are always related to their commitment to their families. Her study also showed

---

14. Glanville, "Leadership Development," 259.

15. Glanville, 262.

16. Glanville, 262–263.

17. Glanville, 265.

18. Glanville, 259.

19. Glanville, 259–260.

20. Glanville, 212–214.

21. Glanville, 265.

that being a wife and mother who is supported by her husband and children is crucial for effective ministry.[22]

In addition, Glanville points out that men assume that they can be leaders but women begin from the premise of uncertainty, wondering at the possibility of assuming leadership. The theological environment surrounding American Christian women leaders has a profound impact on their personal perception of the leadership role, their interpretation of a personal ministry call, the availability of leadership ministry opportunities, and the availability and type of mentoring that might be received.[23] Her analysis showed that American women leaders' theological environment changes as their life situation changes: a constant change – mostly from complementarian to egalitarian perspectives. The result reveals that American Christian women leaders respond to their call to ministry leadership in ways that allow them to exercise their gifts effectively. The woman's commitment to her call may be guided by factors such as "inner conviction, encouragement by others, events and opportunities."[24]

Nevertheless, Glanville's work also demonstrates that women's calls to leadership are discouraged and limited by the lack of role models or mentors, lack of significant ministry involvement and various factors in the theological environment, and that the delay between the women's sense of call into leadership and the pursuit of that call is more evident for women than for men. This delay is attributed to the theological environment, and to differences in their commitment to their family and their understanding of their own identity as a leader called to serve. Appropriate mentoring would help women pursue their call to leadership by providing opportunities for honest dialogue about their theological environment, supporting their creation of visions for leadership and ministry, and encouraging and drawing attention to further opportunities for leadership.[25]

Clinton's and Glanville's ideas influenced my interpretation of the development of leaders, God's shaping activities, and the challenges of, and obedience to, the leadership call to ministry seen in the ten Asian Christian women servant-leaders' narratives.

---

22. Glanville, 265.
23. Glanville, 261.
24. Glanville, 261–263.
25. Glanville, 263–265.

Challenges Encountered by Christian Leaders

Challenges are expected in leadership growth. Christian leaders can expect to encounter challenges such as compromise, ambition, impossible situations, failure and jealousy. These challenges can be overcome: compromise is overcome by integrity; personal ambition is overcome by a genuine concern for God's glory.

If, according to Glanville, the theological environment shapes American Christian women leaders' perceptions, it may be that Asian Christian women are also challenged by their theological environment. A brief introduction to complementarian, egalitarian and feminist theology sets the background so that the women's narratives can be better appreciated.

There are rewards for the path of obedience taken by Christian servant-leaders – relationships, legacies, intimacy with God, a Christ-like image, the opportunity to invest in another life and the crown of life (Rev 2:10).

Challenges to Spiritual Growth

Any situation that causes doubt and challenges faith in God has the potential to strengthen faith in God. Failure is not final – it is a stepping-stone to success. Addressing pitfalls as challenges, Henry and Richard Blackaby assert that pride, sexual sin, cynicism, greed, mental laziness, oversensitivity, spiritual lethargy, domestic neglect, administrative carelessness and remaining in a position too long may affect leaders unless they are in sync with God's Spirit.

Pride, the leader's worst enemy, allows leaders to see themselves as better and greater and take God's glory for themselves. Proud leaders are not teachable and turn away from God's guidance; leaders negate God's work and blessings in their lives when they think that they have enough talent, wisdom and charisma to achieve their goals. Pride leaves little space for love or compassion and inevitably leaders make God their opponent. Sexual sin, on the other hand, affects and destroys careers, families and reputations – of individuals and of the Christian community. Christian leaders are accountable and should practice what they preach, consider the results of sexual sin and maintain a strong, intimate walk with Jesus.[26]

Christian leaders can overcome challenges in three ways. First, leaders must have a "healthy awareness of the pitfalls that can bring failure and disgrace

---

26. Blackaby and Blackaby, *Spiritual Leadership*, 313–346.

to leaders"; second, leaders need to put "safeguards in place that will provide protection in times of temptation or indecision"; third, leaders should always remember that people matter more than productivity, that leaders are not indispensable and that "the most effective, efficient thing they can do for their organization is to maintain a close, vibrant relationship with God."[27]

The Cost of Leadership

Andrew Le Peau, in "The High Cost of Leadership," groups the costs of leadership into three categories: physical, emotional and spiritual. Time and money are physical costs; conflicts, fears of the "unknown" and loneliness are emotional costs; spiritual costs are spiritual attacks – the consequences of sexual temptation and pride.[28] Whatever the cost of leadership, Christian servant-leaders are exhorted to sacrifice their self-interests, and to carry their crosses and lay down their lives as Jesus did (1 John 3:16).

Le Peau suggests six ways spiritual leaders can counter the costs of leadership and serve well: being a part of support groups; being a part of accountability groups; clinging onto their sense of God's calling; studying, obeying and resting in God's Word; knowing effective ways to respond to personal sinful behavior; and recognizing their spiritual poverty before God.[29]

Generally, leaders in Asian Christian society are aware of the costs of leadership. Since most Asian nations are developing nations, leaders understand the need to sacrifice time, effort and money. Asian Christian women leaders recognize that they may have to work twice or three times as hard as their male peers to be recognized in patriarchal societies.

The ten women in this book have gone through various challenges such as persecution, lack of recognition and discouragement, and have overcome them.

Rewards Gained by Servant-Leaders

All leaders – and especially Christian leaders – pay a price; there is a cost for becoming a servant-leader. However, faithful servant-leaders who have been obedient to God can expect to receive heavenly rewards (Luke 18:28–30); they know that they have accomplished their divine calling.

---

27. Blackaby and Blackaby, 347–348.
28. Le Peau, "High Cost," para. 2.
29. Le Peau, paras. 20–24.

While Sanders encourages Christian leaders to be ambitious about achieving God's will for their lives, he also reminds them that true spiritual leaders receive rewards through their relationships: a spiritually mature family; favor from colleagues; and a variety of friendships with people from diverse ethnic backgrounds. Christian leaders leave behind a legacy in three main areas: in their families, when children and grandchildren continue in the ministry; in their work life when, because of their leadership skills, the workplace becomes a better place or the society has been affected positively by the influence of these godly leaders; and in God's kingdom, when they seek God's kingdom and his righteousness first (Matt 6:33).[30]

Swindoll echoes Sanders' thoughts in his meditation on Micah 6:8. He asserts first that, through a life that honors God, believers develop the strong character of Christ as they pursue justice, kindness and humility.[31] Second, when their personal conscience remains untainted and in close communion with God, believers enjoy relief, freedom and joy. Third, believers who walk in faith and obedience experience intimacy with God. Fourth, believers who walk in godly ways have the privilege of being mentors – having the opportunity to shape another life is a significant reward. Fifth, they have a reward worth waiting for: the crown of life at the end of their lives. Finally, in contrast to Sanders, for Swindoll, the legacy of believers is their character and attitudes.[32]

In Asian society, individuals receive rewards – usually money or recognition – only when they do exceptionally well in their work or studies. In the course of mingling with full-time female pastors in a Southeast Asian country, I often heard the lament, "We work so hard but our salaries are not as high as for the male pastors." They were not complaining but stating a very discriminative fact in the church system. These female pastors have not allowed the disparity in wages to block their path to service excellence in the kingdom of God.

Women in Christian Servant-Leadership: Ongoing Tensions

Glanville states that the "woman's theological environment impacts a woman's perception of her potential role in ministry, the way she understands and perceives her call into ministry, the opportunities available to her, and the

30. Sanders, *Spiritual Leadership*, 351–370.
31. Swindoll, "The Rewards."
32. Swindoll, "The Rewards."

mentoring and encouragement she is likely to receive in her pursuit of ministry."[33]

Egalitarians start from the premise that as both male and female are created in the image of God (Gen 1:28), they are also equally able to minister according to their gifts and that the church assembly should be without any gender bias in ministry or leadership positions.[34] John Piper and Wayne Grudem argue that, though complementarians also accept male and female equality in the image of God, they understand the Scriptures to restrict key church and family leadership roles to qualified male leaders and husbands respectively. Piper and Grudem add that, in their view, evangelical feminists have misinterpreted the scriptural truths regarding biblical manhood and womanhood and as a consequence have contributed to churchmen and women's confusion about their own roles.[35]

The Controversy

How many times have you heard of a gifted female pastor or preacher who was not able to serve as a preacher at a Sunday service or was confined to leading the children and/or women's ministries? In the mission fields of Asia and Africa, I have had the pleasure of serving congregations at their Sunday services, prayer vigils, retreats and local conferences for close to two decades. However, within my previous organization, I was given *one* opportunity to preach at a dawn prayer service. Some male pastors and church leaders were surprised that I was able to exposit the Word accurately and came to congratulate me on this achievement. I was not surprised to receive such a joyful reception from the pastors and leaders. They may have never heard a theologically educated but unordained (at that time) female servant-leader with the experience of preaching in many churches for more than a decade. It was a pleasant surprise for them. As for me, it is what I do in the mission field regularly and therefore not a surprise to be invited to teach or preach the Word.

The idea that women can be servant-leaders in churches and ministries continues to be a controversial issue in the Asian context as some Christians believe that leadership is reserved for men only. This debate continues into

---

33. Glanville, "Leadership Development," 57.

34. Glanville, 58.

35. Piper and Grudem, *Recovering*, 10.

the twenty-first century despite biblical and historical evidence of Christian women in leadership roles.

In his foreword to L. E. Maxwell's *Women in Ministry*, Ted Randall cites an untitled poem by an anonymous author:

> We men, we are the stronger sex –
> It always has been so!
> We send our gifts to mission fields
> To which the women go!
>
> While up the steepest jungle paths,
> A woman bravely treads,
> We men who are of the stronger sex,
> Just pray beside our beds.
> While women leave to go abroad
> The heathen souls to reach,
> We men, who are the stronger sex,
> Just stay at home to preach.
>
> While women in some far-off shack
> Do brave the flies and the heat,
> We men, who are the stronger sex,
> In cool and comfort eat.
> Fatigued and weary, needing rest,
> The women battle on,
> We men, who are the stronger sex,
> Just write and cheer them on.
> O valiant men – come let us sleep
> And rest our weary heads,
> We shall not be the stronger sex
>
> If we neglect our beds![36]

Maxwell sought to "justify women's privilege and liberty to participate in public ministry."[37]

This is the irony found in the Western theological environment. The complementarian theological environment particularly in American society dictates that it is fine for women to continue to be sent out to the mission

---

36. Anonymous, as cited in Maxwell, *Women in Ministry*, 9–10.
37. Maxwell, 13.

field while men "stay at home to preach." "At home," the women are denied leadership and sometimes pastoral leadership, but in the mission field, they can be disciple-makers, pastors, church-planters, deliverers, or prophetesses.

An Introduction to Complementarian Thought

Kevin Higham challenges the question "What is the role of women in leadership?" and proposes a replacement question that is more positive towards women as leaders: "What do we do with women leaders?"[38] In his exploration of the understanding of "women in leadership" with three women and a male pastor from Western churches, Higham was not surprised by the traditionalist [complementarian] women's response: they did not expect women to participate in church governmental leadership. He was not surprised by the traditionalist [complementarian] pastor's definitive view that "biblical" submission to 1 Corinthians 14, 1 Timothy 2 and Titus 2 requires that no woman serve in church governmental leadership.[39] In contrast, the egalitarian view is that in Christ Jesus women are free to pursue leadership and to be all that they can be. Higham's findings are similar to those of Glanville, Groothuis, Cunningham and Hamilton:[40] the definition of a woman and her role dictated by society, church tradition and scriptural interpretation has had an impact and remains a key determinant for the Christian woman's understanding of her leadership role. Higham concedes: "Regardless of which view we hold, ultimately our concern must be for the pastoral well-being of the women involved . . . My apprehension is that in doing battle for the 'correct stance' we actually overlook the very people whom we are aiming to address; the women themselves, thereby causing many casualties, and injuries to the women in the process."[41]

Brief Description of Complementarian Thought

Complementarians believe that, although both male and female are made in the image of God, nevertheless from the beginning, at their creation, God ordered their relationship for all time: first man, then woman. Their belief centers on the understanding that men and women are created differently to

---

38. Higham, "Questioning the Question!," 89.

39. Higham, 89–91.

40. Glanville, "Leadership Development"; Groothuis in Pierce, Groothuis and Fee, "Contemporary Evangelicals"; Cunningham and Hamilton, *Why Not Women?*

41. Higham, "Questioning the Question!," 92.

function in specific complementary roles.[42] They are convinced that "women are equal before God in worth, value, but not before men when it comes to who is in charge of things."[43]

Piper and Grudem state that the primary responsibility for Christ-like leadership and teaching in the church and family responsibilities of leadership, protection and provision belongs to the man. These complementarian authors strongly believe that it is unbiblical for women to take on the role of a pastor or elder in the church, and, while in a marriage, the wife should be a model of submission to her husband.[44]

The Male Voice as Authority in the Church and Women's Role as Helpers

There is no opposition to the use of the teaching or prophecy gifts by women. Quoting 1 Timothy 2:12, Piper and Grudem argue that the "teaching inappropriate for a woman is the teaching of men in settings or ways that dishonor the calling of men to bear the primary responsibility of teaching and leadership. This primary responsibility is to be carried out by [male] pastors and elders."[45]

They strongly emphasize that, from their understanding of Scripture, Christian men are the only persons authorized to hold the offices of pastors and elders,[46] and that there is no leeway for women to take on pastoral positions or eldership even under the authority of the male pastor.[47] Complementarian thinkers refer to 1 Timothy 2:12 – "I do not permit a woman to teach or to exercise authority over a man; rather, she is to remain quiet" – to support this view.

The "traditional interpretation" of the above verse "forbids women to teach or make decisions."[48] According to Kroeger and Kroeger various assumptions undergird complementarian thinking in relation to this verse. The first assumption is that Eve was a secondary creation: she was created after man and, therefore, inferior to men.[49] The second assumption is that Eve and women like Eve are "gullible and easily deceived" and therefore cannot be leaders or

---

42. Glanville, "Leadership Development," 58.
43. Groothuis, *Good News for Women*, 26–27.
44. Piper and Grudem, *Recovering*, 56–57.
45. Piper and Grudem, 64.
46. Piper and Grudem, 56.
47. Piper and Grudem, 64.
48. Kroeger and Kroeger, *I Suffer Not*, 17.
49. Kroeger and Kroeger, 17.

teachers as they are "often led astray."[50] The third assumption is that Eve was "primarily responsible for original sin."[51] Complementarians refer to 1 Timothy 2:14 – "Adam was not deceived, but the woman was deceived and became a transgressor" – to support this view. The fourth assumption is that women bear Eve's guilt for turning against God.[52]

Some Christian women view leadership of women in a different light. Presbyterian church leaders Susan Hunt and Peggy Hutcheson believe that the female population in churches remains an untapped resource, that the church has not recognized women's gifts and freed them to exercise these gifts. Confusion and tension build in churches where male leaders make the decisions while, paradoxically, women are allowed to make decisions for their employers and in their homes. The authors suggest that while women acknowledge that they are created differently, they also embrace the fact that God created them to be helpers (Gen 2:18), and the fact that God is our helper demonstrates that being a helper is not a weaker or lesser role. In this way, Christian women can "un-confuse" themselves and focus on their reason for being created to be helpers (Isa 43:6b–7) and that, as helpers in God's image, they are created to be servant-leaders.[53]

Piper and Grudem indicate that the biblical women whom egalitarians often use as examples of co-leaders in the ministry of the apostle Paul should be seen as co-workers and not as leaders, as there is no indication that these women were leaders who had authority over men. They argue, for example, that while Euodia and Syntyche in Philippians 4:2–3 are honored as laborers working with the apostle Paul, "there are no compelling grounds for affirming that the nature of the ministry was contrary" to the limitations set out in 1 Timothy 2:12.[54]

An Introduction to Egalitarian Thought

Egalitarian thought operates out of a sense of justice and the conviction that "the traditional order which has been imposed on women and men is not in keeping with God's will for His people."[55] Fee makes a similar point to

---

50. Kroeger and Kroeger, 18.
51. Kroeger and Kroeger, 20.
52. Kroeger and Kroeger, *I Suffer Not*, 21–23.
53. Hunt and Hutcheson, *Leadership for Women*, 29–30.
54. Piper and Grudem, *Recovering*, 62–64.
55. Groothuis, *Good News for Women*, 210.

Glanville[56] in underlining that what "is at stake is not whether all people are equally gifted; they are not. What is at stake is whether God the Holy Spirit, in His gifting the people of God, ever makes gender a prior requirement for certain kinds of gifting."[57] The Holy Spirit's authority must be recognized so that gifted women operate in their leadership gifting. The long-standing emphasis and problem of male seminarians thinking that they qualify for ministry because of their gender would be alleviated.[58] Finally, and most importantly, Fee states that having a woman in leadership "opens the door to the possibility that ministry is a two-way street . . . The New Testament evidence is that the Holy Spirit is gender inclusive, gifting both men and women, and thus potentially setting the whole body free for all the many parts to minister and in various ways to give leadership to others."[59]

Rebecca Groothuis asks, "Why should the male be given the voice of authority in spiritual matters and the female silenced and subordinated before the male's authority?"[60] God did put women in authority and the scriptural evidence includes Miriam (Exod 15:20; Mic 6:4), Deborah (Judg 4–5), Huldah (2 Kgs 22:14–20; 2 Chr 34:11–33), Noadiah (Neh 6:14), the wife of the prophet Isaiah (Isa 8:3), Anna (Luke 2:36), Phoebe (Rom 16:1–2), the women at the empty grave (Matt 28:1–10; Mark 16:1–7; Luke 24:1–10; John 20:11–18), the four daughters of Philip (Acts 21:8–9), Priscilla (Rom 16:3–5; 1 Cor 16:19; Acts 18:24–26) and Junia (Rom 16:7). God alone gives spiritual leadership, but some Christians have regarded female Bible characters' authority and leadership as a "bizarre blip, less authoritative than that of men."[61]

Finding scriptural support that frees women to rise above themselves to become all that they can be – and especially leaders – in their God-given ministries is a logical response to this ongoing tension regarding Christian women in leadership. Hamilton determines that in relation to women, Jesus has no double standards: he makes no exclusions and sets no limits on their God-given destiny. Women were a part of the ministry of Jesus, as established in the Gospels, and women were also a part of Paul's ministry, as recorded in Romans 16 and in the other epistles.[62]

---

56. Glanville, "Leadership Development," 88, 95.

57. Fee, "Priority of Spirit Gifting," 241.

58. Fee, 254.

59. Fee, 254.

60. Groothuis, *Good News for Women*, 189.

61. Groothuis, 189–207.

62. Hamilton, "Jesus Broke," 112–128.

Groothuis states firmly her lack of surprise that "the church historically has looked to secular culture for guidance" as "patriarchy did not originate with the Judeo-Christian culture."[63]

Hamilton, in the chapter "Jesus Broke Down the Walls," relates the story of the woman in the crowd who blessed Jesus by blessing the mother who had given birth to him and nursed him (Luke 11:27–28), and argues that this reflects the "traditional rabbinic position: women receive God's blessing indirectly through their menfolk, their sons and husbands."[64] Hamilton argues that when Jesus responds by countering that those who obey the word of God will be blessed, he (Jesus) is effectively "rejecting the system of thought that for centuries had cut women off from active participation in the things of God. Jesus would have no part in religious values that relegated, exempted, excluded, and limited a person's walk with God and her ministry for God . . . The new standard was personal obedience to God."[65]

In addition, when the apostle Paul mentions "Euodia and Syntyche," he refers to them as women "who have labored side by side with me in the gospel together with Clement and the rest of my fellow workers, whose names are in the book of life" (Phil 4:2–3). When the apostle wrote to the Roman church circa 50 CE, he included greetings from a large team who had been working alongside him, naming Phoebe, Prisca, Mary and Junia; Junia, in particular, is commended as a fellow apostle (Rom 16:1–7).

St Paul insists "there is neither Jew nor Greek, there is neither slave nor free, there is no male and female, for you are all one in Christ Jesus" (Gal 3:28). He reminds us again in Ephesians 2:11–22 that Jesus is the "peace that has broken down the wall of hostility." In this letter Paul also reminds us that the possibility of having one Spirit can only be ours in and through Christ. While this passage refers to Jews and Gentiles, the principle of oneness applies to a community that clearly divides leadership roles according to gender. Paul argues that in Jesus Christ, men and women are not hostile, they are at peace; they are not aliens but family members of the same household, and that both men and women are "being built together into a dwelling place for God by the Spirit" (Eph 2:22).

Jesus has broken down the walls and is gender inclusive, asserting that both men and women who follow him are qualified to serve him in the expansion

---

63. Groothius, *Good News for Women*, 1.

64. Hamilton, "Jesus Broke," 127.

65. Hamilton, 127–128.

of the kingdom. While egalitarian writers demonstrate that Asian Christian women can rise up in spiritual leadership according to the Spirit's gifting, revelation and guidance, a more significant reason for their doing so is the unity that God desires for his people. The women's narratives in this book reveal that some women are affected by the theological interpretation of Bible passages related to women and leadership or by a challenge they need to manage or overcome as they obey their God-given call to servant-leadership in ministry.

An Introduction to Asian Feminist Theological Thought

The strong influences of theology and hermeneutics in Asia are seen throughout the beginnings of Asian Church history through Western colonization and missionary endeavors. History records that the gospel arrived on Asian shores through Western missionary efforts, trade and settlements. Asian Church history began with Christ, the apostles, Marco Polo, Gregory the Illuminator and many Western foreigners who were invited into the courts of kings. Some of these early believers were martyred for their unshakeable faith in Christ.[66]

Asians view Christianity as a Western religion, rather than appreciating the reality that Christianity began in Asia with an Asian man. For example, in reference to Singapore, Professor Robbie Goh from the National University of Singapore writes: "Christianity (unlike religions with a traditional racial association such as Islam with the Malays, and Buddhism, Taoism and traditional Chinese practices with the Chinese) is also seen as a religion associated with 'outside' or 'Western' cultural influences, one which is obliged to grow its community of adherents at the expense of one of the other race-based religions."[67]

The consequence in the Asian theological literary community is that there are very few Asian theologians, writers of theology or experts in feminist theology. This is evidenced by the lack of related literature from Asian perspectives.

Asian feminist theology has its own challenges as Asian Christians consciously try not to view it as an extension of Western feminist theology – first, Asia's challenge is that it does not have a common language, and second, there is a lack of literary resources related to Asian feminist theology.[68]

---

66. Moffett, *History*.
67. Goh, "Christian Identities."
68. Chakkalakal, "Asian Women," 29.

Overview of Feminism and Feminist Theology from Western Perspectives

The roots of feminism in Asia can be traced back to Western origins. The feminist movement is more than a century old.[69] In particular, Janette Hassey's investigation of women's roles in fundamentalist circles a century ago through the lives of key evangelicals and fundamentalists revealed that fundamentalism "was neither exclusively male nor inherently antifeminist."[70] Evangelical women have openly established Bible institutes, mission agencies, and served as pastors, teachers and evangelists since the late 1800s in the United States of America.[71]

Western feminist theologians acknowledge that there are different types of feminism. Riswold, for example, describes feminism in its various forms: Marxist, socialist, liberal, radical, cultural and gynocentric.

According to Riswold, Marxist feminists are concerned with critiquing capitalism, while socialist feminists locate women's oppression within the economic system; liberal feminists posit that women's oppression is a result of the unequal treatment of women in the legal system, and therefore they seek justice and social change; radical feminists view gender oppression as basic and the fundamental form of oppression; cultural feminists aim to endorse again what patriarchy has devalued after re-examination of gender differences; gynocentric feminists push for separatism because they view gender differences as extremely significant; difference feminism is a lesser form of radical feminism in that the feminists remain neutral in relation to separatism and they seek to explain the gender differences.[72]

In the evangelical sector of Christian faith, some people today may agree that the terms "evangelical" and "feminist" are non-contradictory, but it did not begin this way. The term "evangelical feminism" was coined in 1974 by a group of evangelicals who gathered to explore the topic of women's equality. As such, the "biblical feminist" or "evangelical feminist" concluded, "when interpreted correctly, the Bible teaches equality of women and men."[73]

Feminist theology is then observed as a form of contextual theology whereby "women [are] refusing to be controlled by definitions of who and what they should be."[74] In other words, "feminism criticizes sexism and patriarchy,

---

69. Park, "The Contribution," 187.

70. Hassey, "Evangelical Women," 40.

71. Hassey, 40–41.

72. Riswold, *Feminism and Christianity*, 9.

73. Cochran, *Evangelical Feminism*, 1–2.

74. Isherwood and McEwan, *Introducing Feminist Theology*, 9.

and advocates for the equal humanity of women."[75] Watson defines feminist theology thus: "Feminist theology is the critical, contextual, constructive, and creative re-reading and re-writing of Christian theology. It regards women – and their bodies, perspectives and experiences – as relevant to the agenda of Christian theologians and advocates them as subjects of theological discourses and as full citizens of the church."[76]

According to Riswold, feminism seeks to embrace both men and women with a view to benefiting them culturally.[77] For example, the rise of women in leadership is attributed to feminism's impact on Christianity.[78] Since the 1800s, evangelical feminists, both men and women, have been actively involved in defending the call and need for women to speak in public under the guidance of the Holy Spirit, for women's ordination,[79] and have advocated the public ministry of women.[80]

Western feminism's engagement with Christian theology seems to expose "the idolatry of projecting onto God false dualisms or hierarchical arrangements between men and women, spirit and matter . . . It also exposes the profoundly harmful effects of patriarchy on the humanity of both men and women . . . and rejects patriarchy's hold upon society and church."[81]

Ronald Pierce states that contemporary evangelicals in support of gender equality remain divided on the term "evangelical feminist":

> They affirmed the essentials of their theologically conservative background, especially the inspiration and authority of the Scripture, while arguing that restrictive roles for women do not reflect an accurate interpretation of the texts. Evangelicals . . . were united in their opposition to the more radical religious and secular forms of feminism, yet they remained divided on the "evangelical feminist" question.[82]

---

75. Riswold, *Feminism and Christianity*, 4.

76. Watson, *Feminist Theology*, 2–3.

77. Riswold, *Feminism and Christianity*, 70.

78. Riswold, 72.

79. Hassey, "Evangelical Women," 43–45. Frances Willard (1839–1898) wrote *Women in the Pulpit* in 1988. B. T. Roberts wrote *Ordaining Women* in 1891 and fought for women's ordination in the Free Methodist denomination.

80. Fredrik Franson wrote *Prophesying Daughters* in response to criticism of his support for women evangelists, while A. J. Gordon wrote *The Ministry of Women* in 1894 to present scriptural support for women's preaching.

81. LaCugna, *God for Us*, 3.

82. Pierce, "Contemporary Evangelicals," 58.

In summary, Western feminist theology is a contextual and creative reading of Christian theology pertaining to women with a view to helping them uncover the destructive consequences of patriarchy for both men and women. However, not all evangelical women appreciate being termed "evangelical feminists," even though they might defend the extensive roles for women in ministry through biblical exegesis.

Feminist Theology from Asian Perspectives

Yong Tong Jin, a former coordinator of culture and theology for the Asian Women's Resource Center, points out that with the rise of feminism "a new wave of women's consciousness swept through Asia" in the late 1970s and 1980s as a response to oppression.[83] Indian Catholic nun and biblical scholar Pauline Chakkalakal sees it as a fight by women against patriarchal dictatorship, as "resistance to all forms of violence" by women, and women challenging "oppressive and discriminatory attitudes."[84] The "deconstructing and reconstructing of theology and women envisioning a new heaven and earth"[85] are part of the re-awakening of Asian women's consciousness.[86]

Chakkalakal's Indian perspective is that Indian women are involved in economic and social struggles. This includes feminist movements that are struggling against patriarchy. Patriarchy is defined as a social system of male supremacy and control that permeates and dominates culture and religion in Asia. Women's struggle against patriarchy is focused on "their rightful place in family and society."[87] Indian women especially find strength in their solidarity. Economic liberation for women's empowerment is still insufficient and continues to evade Indian women.[88]

Referring to the rise of hundreds of women's organizations in the Philippines, Chakkalakal claims that Asian Christian women have drawn their inspiration from such organizations and challenged patriarchy in religious institutions, and that these women seek to define Asian feminist theology. However, Asian women are encouraged to give authenticity to theology by their participation in movements for political action and social transformation, by networking with other women's organizations at every level and by ensuring

---

83. Jin, "On Being Church," 109.
84. Chakkalakal, "Asian Women," 23.
85. Chakkalakal, 23.
86. Jin, "On Being Church," 109.
87. Chakkalakal, "Asian Women," 24–26.
88. Gajiwala, "Power Struggles," 51–57.

that Asian women consciously shift their anti-patriarchal mindset to that of living life by involving themselves in the lives of others.[89]

While Yong and Chakkalakal see feminism as a theological concern, Korean Christian author Park Bokyoung approaches it as a missiological concern. According to Park's doctor of philosophy dissertation, where she discusses the contributions of Korean Christian women to the Church at large and missions, missiological feminism is characterized by:

1. Freedom in reconciliation whereby the vertical relationship with God and horizontal relationships with people encourage freedom and equality.

2. Justice and solidarity with the oppressed whereby transformation arises from a genuine encounter with Christ.

3. Unity in Christ between male and female and attempts to regain the image of God within the community, which then become crucial strategies in the full engagement of God's mission.[90]

Even as Park attempts to regain the image of God through unity between male and female in Christ, another Korean pastor (of the Women's Church in Korea) and feminist theologian, Sook-Ja Chung, views her own understanding of Korean feminist theology and especially her ordination as a pastor as a signal to "break down the walls of hierarchy such as ordination, sacredness, privilege, clericalism . . .,"[91] but Chung's efforts in her Presbyterian church were geared towards building a women's ministry that would promote equality in relationships. Chung also equates her community ministry to feminist ministry whereby, in her church, women who are seen as oppressed engage in a liberation that pushes them to a platform of equality with men.[92]

Summary

The preparation of Christian leaders is viewed from a Western perspective because there has not been any extensive study of leadership from an Asian perspective. The discussion introduces leadership emergence theories from both Western male and female perspectives, and the concept of the costs

---

89. Chakkalakal, "Asian Women," 28–33.
90. Park, "The Contribution," 195.
91. Chung, "Women Church," 73.
92. Chung, 73–81.

of leadership. While Christian servant-leaders can expect to face spiritual, emotional and physical challenges – costs of leadership – their obedience to Jesus at all costs is more than rewarded by the ongoing manifestations of God's presence and the legacy they leave after their death, a legacy that touches many lives.

The introduction to the ongoing tensions and controversies surrounding women in Christian leadership facilitates the reader's understanding of complementarian, egalitarian and feminist perspectives on women's leadership in the church.

While advocates of all perspectives possess and find common ground in their earnest desire to love and serve God in the best way possible, their understanding of scriptural passages shapes their ideas about women in leadership. The complementarian advocate believes that women are not allowed to teach, preach or pastor men or be ordained as pastors and deacons. Some advocates share a middle ground with the egalitarian camp whereby they accept women's ordination and leadership as deacons but do not permit them to teach, preach to and pastor men. Egalitarians approach Scripture with an understanding that both men and women should be encouraged to use their gifts and talents for the advancement of God's kingdom. Both genders are capable and gifted to pursue leadership in various capacities, including those of deacons and pastors, according to their call. Feminist theologians are concerned with the empowerment of women and work hard to deliver women from their patriarchal suppression. Asian feminist theology, especially, seems to support the rise of women's groups and organizations to challenge Asian patriarchy that permeates every environment.

5

Re-narrating the Narratives

I have had personal and direct access or contact over a period of five to twenty years with at least nine of the women introduced in this book. Therefore, they shared their Christian leadership experiences without any reservations. I shared church membership with three of the four Singaporeans (Lydia, Pushpamani, Kat), and I studied at Singapore Bible College with the fourth Singaporean (Alice). The two Koreans (Young Kim, Kim Cho) were my colleagues in South Korea, and two Indians (Priscilla, Ruth) were my disciples. I befriended the Malaysian Iban pastor (Elizabeth) when I served the Iban people from 1995 to 2001 through short-term ministry trips. A male Jordanian colleague introduced me to RA, the Jordanian servant-leader. RA was the only one whom I did not know prior to our interaction.

All are members of Protestant churches throughout Asia, are over thirty-five years old and are active in ministry in Christian environments as leaders. They represent various Protestant denominations, including Anglican, Baptist, Methodist and Presbyterian, whose beliefs are perceived to be evangelical. At least six women also represent para-church organizations. They are from North Asia (South Korea), South Asia (India), Southeast Asia (Singapore and Malaysia) and West Asia (Middle East). All had received education up to at least senior high school (American terminology) or secondary level (British terminology). Though they all speak English, the Malaysian servant-leader used English and *Bahasa Melayu*, her native tongue, in her narrative; as I am literate in *Bahasa Melayu*, I was able to understand her very well.

As my ministry travels to various nations in Asia allowed me to meet the women who would be willing to share their life stories, I used convenience sampling to collect potential interviewees. I used purposive sampling to select Asian Christian women leaders from a specific population (that is, Asian Christian women leaders residing in an Asian nation) who would be able to tell me about their salvation experiences, their growth into leadership, the challenges in their leadership experiences and their approaches to overcoming leadership challenges.

Both sampling methods have limitations. Purposive sampling is limited as the sample of Asian Christian women leaders may not represent other Asian Christian women leaders who belong to non-Protestant religious backgrounds, or who come from tribes where matriarchal lineage is important, or who are the children or wives from polygamous relationships, or who might be illiterate or have less theological training. In convenience sampling, the partiality is related to how the potential sample is selected. Nine of the women were Asian Christian women leaders I had met or knew through previous shared ministry and educational experiences. These women are representative of women I have discipled or ministered alongside in Asia. These women volunteered or agreed to be interviewed and allowed their voices to be heard. While my sampling methods mean my findings are not easily generalized, the stories I collected serve the purpose of giving voice to Asian Christian women servant-leaders' experiences from salvation to service. Russell Bernard's discussion of convenience and purposive sampling argues that "All samples represent *something*. The trick is to make them representative of what you want them to be. That's what turns a convenience sample into a purposive one."[1]

For example, in sharing her story, RA, a Jordanian Christian woman servant-leader of Arab origin, provided me with a first-hand personal understanding of her Middle Eastern community. As I was on vacation and had the opportunity to meet RA for a limited time (one and a half hours), I turned this "convenience sample into a purposive one,"[2] with her permission, by including an Arab voice in this book.

Unstructured interviewing is one way of gathering information and attaching descriptive meaning to events in individuals' lives.[3] I used semi-structured interview questions to explore and illuminate the personal stories and experiences of interviewees:

1. How does the Asian context shape opportunities and challenges for Asian evangelical Christian women leaders?

    a. How and when did you come to accept Christ as Lord and Savior?

    b. When did you step into leadership?

---

1. Bernard, *Research Methods*, 184.

2. Bernard, 184.

3. Burns, *Introduction*, 388.

c. When did you become a Christian leader?

d. How has your cultural background helped or hindered you in developing as a leader?

e. How did you manage hindrances to your development as a leader?

2. What are the biblical principles for Asian evangelical Christian women in servant-leadership?

a. What are some of your thoughts about servant-leadership?

3. What is Christian leadership for Asian evangelical Christian women?

4. What is your definition of Christian leadership?

5. What are the positive developmental patterns for Asian evangelical Christian women in servant-leadership?

a. Who are/were some of your encouragers as you stepped into and developed in leadership?

b. What did they say or do to encourage you to develop as a leader?

c. How else did you prepare yourself for leadership responsibilities?

6. What are the key opportunities and challenges for Asian evangelical Christian women as they develop as servant-leaders?

7. What are/were some of your ministry responsibilities as a Christian leader?

8. What are some of the challenges you encountered as a Christian leader?

9. What advice do you have for emerging Christian women leaders?

The personal stories and experiences of these Christian women servant-leaders demonstrate and verify their impact on other people or situations. In fact, I took the narrative inquiry and analysis approach to further understand the experiences of these women. In addition, I coined two terms – "host nation" and "home nation" – to define the location of these women.[4] The "host nation"

---

4. As an illustration of "host nation" and "home nation": Ruth is South Indian in nationality and origin but has lived in a Middle Eastern nation for more than a decade. In Ruth's case, her home nation is India and her host nation is the Middle Eastern nation. An alternative example is Pushpamani: her host and home nations are the same – Singapore.

is the country where the interviewees reside, while the "home nation" is the country of birth.

Narrative Inquiry and Analysis

Catherine Riessman asks, "What is different about narrative studies, compared to ethnographic accounts and recent approaches to textual analysis?"[5] In response to her own question, she cites Rosenwald and Ochberg's observation that, in ethnographic research, it is the "events, not the stories informants create about them, that are intended to command our attention"; narratives are studied through systematic interpretation of the interviewee's interpretation; narrative inquiry and analysis would be a suitable approach for studies dealing with subjectivity and identity.[6] Webster and Mertova also claim that "narrative inquiry is set in human stories of experience . . . Narrative is well suited to addressing complexities and subtleties of human experiences in teaching and learning."[7]

Narrative analysis is an observation of how individuals make sense of the actions and events in their life narratives. Narratives are representations of individuals' lives and require their narrators to interpret them.[8]

Narrative inquiry demands that the interpretation be accurate but this depends on literary practices and reader responses. Personal narratives, especially, require that the researcher "create and recreate voices over and over again during the research process."[9]

Re-checking the interpretation with the original narrator is advisable as meanings can shift as the consciousness of the narrator changes. "In the final analysis, the work is ours. We have to take responsibility for its truths."[10]

Steps to Analyzing Narratives

Narrative inquiry and analysis involves five levels of representation in relation to the experience:

---

5. Riessman, *Narrative Analysis*, 4.
6. Rosenwald and Ochberg, *Storied Lives*, 2, cited in Riessman, *Narrative Analysis*, 4.
7. Webster and Mertova, *Using Narrative Inquiry*, 1.
8. Riessman, *Narrative Analysis*, 1–5.
9. Riessman, 16.
10. Riessman, 66–67.

1. Attending – the narrator engages in selective remembering, reflecting on and recollecting events in order to make the experience meaningful.

2. Telling – the narrator projects the meaningful experience to audiences using language that allows listeners to be transported into that particular experience. When listeners begin to ask questions or encourage the narrator to tell more, both parties begin to produce a narrative together. The meaning of the narrative can shift according to the language used, the target audience and the level of interaction.

3. Transcribing – the audio-recording or video-recording of the verbal exchange between listener and storyteller is re-presented[11] in written form.

4. Analyzing – the transcription is analyzed. This is the researcher's defining moment: the researcher scrutinizes the transcript and reshapes the original narrative or narratives in order to interpret and thus re-present the significance of these stories.

5. Reading – readers of the re-shaped and re-presented narratives add their own meanings to the re-shaped narration. When the original narrators read the final product they may or may not recognize the portrayal of their experiences.

These five levels of re-presentation are limited by the contextual meaning created by participants at all five levels.[12]

I began analyzing the narratives while transcribing and spent much time trying to understand the context of the responses, and how I would re-interpret these narratives and lend my voice to the ten voices in this book.

Dynamic Life Engagement through Narrative Inquiry and Analysis

Making observations, conducting interviews and creating a shared environment by retelling stories, bringing them to life and giving them meaning, is an art that demands interpretative skills, imagination and creative writing. The storyteller, writer, transcriber and reader use their understandings of the meaning and nuances in the original story to influence and create these collaborative texts.

---

11. Until the third stage of transcribing, the narrative is generated and performed by the narrator. From the transcribing stage, the narrative is being reproduced by another person.

12. Riessman, 8–15.

In a collective manner, the narrator's experiences of the story become the reality that is re-presented.

Narrative approaches to qualitative research assume that the human participants – interviewees/storytellers, researchers/writers, transcribers, readers – can cross paths with each other through sharing their experiences and imaginations. This crossing of paths facilitates a dynamic engagement of lives that touch each other and hopefully persuade and edify one another. The goal of dynamic life engagement in this context is an improved understanding, for the writer, women and readers, of Asian Christian women leaders' perceptions of Christian leadership, the processes of leadership development, and the challenges to and opportunities for Asian women's servant-leadership. In reading excerpts of their narratives, readers hear the voices of Asian Christian women servant-leaders. In understanding the analysis, readers begin to connect with the meanings communicated through these narratives. And readers may be inspired to question deeply and explore further the issues offered by these narratives.

It is my hope that there will be an increase in the acknowledgment, recognition and restoration of godly, gifted female followers and servant-leaders of Christ in the midst of every Asian Christian congregation.

Engaging with Ethical Issues

In this book, the ten Asian Christian women servant-leaders voice their deepest dreams, hopes, challenges, and disappointments as they share their testimonies of salvation, growth and service as Christian leaders. Such an interaction must involve "mutual respect and integrity."[13]

The National Commission for the Protection of Human Subjects of Biomedical and Behavioral Research issued the "Belmont Report" that outlines three principles of ethical conduct for research with human participants. The researcher has a moral obligation to respect and acknowledge research participants as independent beings and protect those with reduced independent capabilities. The project must demonstrate the principle of beneficence: research participants should experience maximum benefits through their participation. Researchers must treat their participants with justice and fairness.[14]

---

13. Athyal, "Asian Christian Theology," 11.

14. National Commission for the Protection of Human Subjects of Biomedical and Behavioral Research, "The Belmont Report: Ethical Principles and Guidelines for the Protection of Human Subjects in Research" (Washington DC: US Government Publishing Office, 1979);

Protection of Identity

The ten Asian Christian women servant-leaders live in parts of Asia with diverse rules associated with religious issues. For example, freedom of religion is exercised in South Korea; other nations – East Malaysia, India, Jordan, Qatar – are in the category of restricted nations. According to Voice of Martyrs, a Christian organization dedicated to helping persecuted believers and churches around the world, restricted nations "include countries where government policy or practice prevents Christians from obtaining Bibles or other Christian literature . . . where government-sanctioned circumstances or anti-Christian laws lead to Christians being harassed, imprisoned, killed or deprived of possessions and liberties because of their witness."[15] Consequently, it is a researcher's responsibility to offer and maintain confidentiality of information.[16]

The women in this narrative serve in Christian ministries in Australia, China, Ghana, India, Indonesia, Japan, Jordan, Kenya, Kyrgyzstan, Kazakhstan, Malaysia, Nepal, Oman, Pakistan, Qatar, Singapore, South Korea, Sudan and the United States of America.

China, India, Jordan, Kyrgyzstan, Kazakhstan, Malaysia, Nepal, Oman, Pakistan, Qatar and Sudan are identified as restricted nations, while Indonesia, the largest Muslim nation, is considered a hostile nation even though the Indonesian government makes a consistent effort to protect Christian believers when they are attacked and persecuted, as happens frequently.[17]

For Christians whose ministries are located in nations regarded as restricted or highly hostile to the proclamation of the gospel and the work of Christians, it is crucial to keep their identities secret by using pseudonyms or initials; their explicit identification could endanger their lives.

Principle of Beneficence

Information is a valuable commodity: its price is measured in the interviewees' time. Bernard argues that it is unfair if those who share information freely

---

cited in Marczyk, DeMatteo and Festinger, *Essentials*, 237–238.
15. Voice of the Martyrs, "Restricted Nations," para. 2.
16. Marczyk, DeMatteo and Festinger, *Essentials*, 244.
17. Voice of the Martyrs, "Restricted Nations."

receive no payment and the recipients – researchers – are rewarded with money when the research is published.[18]

The ten Asian Christian women leaders voluntarily voiced their experiences of growth as Christians and as leaders in their Christian communities. As openhearted and willing contributors, they did not expect any form of compensation, not even assistance with local transportation. In our interactions, they were extremely supportive and exuded a deep sense of thankfulness to God for redeeming them. My friendships with them allowed me to "reward" them with blessings of prayer.

Environment and Emotions

I interacted with most of the women in their homes or at a mutual friend's home. I met the Jordanian, RA, at her office, and one Singaporean, Alice, at a café in Singapore. During our interactions, we enjoyed each other's company as Christian sisters would – in prayer and fellowship; during the interviews, our sense of freedom allowed us to respond with our emotions. At times, tears flowed freely as we discussed the painful experiences of women struggling to rise up in Christian leadership. At other times, we felt anger at the hurtful remarks of both Christian men and women who doubt women's vision and capabilities. Sometimes, we laughed about funny incidents. With women whom I had discipled, we engaged in thanksgiving because we both saw how God had shaped and directed us as women discipling among the nations.

Summary

The qualitative research process – involving narrative inquiry and analysis – was the process used to discern themes in the dynamic testimonies of Christian women's leadership experiences in an Asian context. Some of the identities of the interviewees remain protected due to their restricted environments where Christian ministry is not welcomed. The Asian Christian women servant-leaders volunteered information and no cash or gift-in-kind transaction, except prayer and blessings, took place. Dynamic life engagement between the two parties evoked strong emotional responses which finally translated to thanksgiving and prayer.

---

18. Bernard, *Research Methods,* 200–202.

6

Daughters of Asia

Let us meet the ten Asian Christian women servant-leaders and begin to learn a little about each one. We will note brief background details such as their cultural backgrounds, salvation experiences, leadership development and current activities.

Daughters of Asia: Personal Information

It is said that women usually do not want anyone to know their ages. But these ten women were more than willing to share their ages, proud to belong to their nations, and did not apologize for being married, widowed or enjoying singlehood. These are confident women in Christ and most were highly educated. They were humbled to be serving in various occupations. One of the best educated and youngest women in this group, Alice, chose to be a homemaker so that she could invest in her children's growth while her husband did the main ministry. However, in my interactions with her, I have noted that she continued to reach out to people whenever the opportunity arose.

Table 1 provides an overview of each woman: ethnicity, marital status, educational qualifications and residence at the time of the interviews.

Daughters of Asia: Spiritual Life Information

Spiritual life information, such as former religious backgrounds, Christian life age, ministry experiences and denomination, is displayed in Table 2. The Christian life ages ranged from twenty to seventy-nine years of journeying with the Lord Jesus Christ. The older Christian will inevitably have more experiences towards personal Christian maturity and growth.

Table 1: Daughters of Asia: Personal Information

Name & Age as at 2015	Ethnicity, Nationality	Marital Status	Education Level, Occupation	Residence
Young Kim, 69	South Korean	Widow	Bachelor degree Author; ministry adviser to Japanese Christians	S. Korea
Kim Cho, 56	South Korean	Married	Doctor of philosophy Missionary teacher	S. Korea
Priscilla, 39	Malayalee Indian	Married	Bachelor degree Tutor	Middle East
Ruth, 39	Malayalee Indian	Married	Science degree Dentist	Middle East
Pushpamani, 86	Indian Singaporean	Married	Teacher's training diploma Homemaker	Singapore
Lydia, 62	Chinese Singaporean	Married	Nursing diploma Homemaker	Singapore
Kat, 54	Chinese Singaporean	Married	Science degree Doctor	Singapore
Alice, 36	Chinese Singaporean	Married	Masters degree Missionary	Central Asia
Elizabeth, 61	Iban Malaysian	Single	Bachelor degree Pastor	Malaysia
RA, 44	Arab Jordanian	Married	Masters degree Founder of non-profit organization	Jordan

Table 2: Daughters of Asia: Spiritual Information

No.	Name	Religious Background	Theological/ Biblical Training; Style*	Ministry Areas	Current Denomination & # of Years as a Christian
1	Young Kim	Christian	Yes; non-formal	1. Author 2. Adviser and founding member of Japanese Christian Fellowship 3. Mother and grandmother	Presbyterian 55
2	Kim Cho	Buddhist	Yes; formal	1. Missionary teacher 2. Researcher 3. Mother	Presbyterian 42
3	Priscilla	Christian	Yes; non-formal	1. Coordinator for South Indian Ministry 2. Facilitator (Bible courses) 3. Preacher 4. Sunday school principal 5. Founding member of fellowship group 6. Mother	Anglican 26
4	Ruth	Syrian Orthodox Christian	Yes; non-formal	1. Facilitator (Bible courses) 2. Preacher 3. Sunday school teacher 4. Mother	Anglican 20

* Non-formal education refers to education and training outside of officially recognized institutions. Informal education refers to lifelong learning of values, skills and attitudes through daily interactions with people and places. Formal training is highly structured and often done within a specified time frame in a recognized institution (Smith, "What Is Non-Formal Education?," paras. 8–10). In the context of this research, non-formal education may be a part of the church ministry or offered by a missions training agency whereby students acquire a diploma or degree through semi-structured programs. In the context of this research, informal education can take place during care group meetings, casual meetings and prayer meetings. In the context of this research, formal biblical/theological education would be offered by Bible colleges or seminaries.

No.	Name	Religious Background	Theological/ Biblical Training; Style	Ministry Areas	Current Denomination & # of Years as a Christian
5	Pushpamani	Christian	Yes; informal	1. Care group leader 2. Prayer leader 3. Evangelist 4. Mother and grandmother	Methodist 79
6	Lydia	Muslim	Yes; formal	1. Counselor to cancer patients 2. Bible teacher 3. Founding member of church plant 4. Mother	Methodist 26
7	Kat	None	Yes; informal	1. Care group leader 2. Church leader 3. Founding member of church plant 4. Mother 5. Grandmother	Methodist 38
8	Alice	Chinese religion	Yes; formal	1. Missionary 2. Mother	Presbyterian 24
9	Elizabeth	Iban tradition and beliefs	Yes; formal	1. Senior pastor 2. District superintendent	Methodist 34
10	RA	Catholic	Yes; informal	1. Founder of non-profit organization serving women 2. Mother	Baptist 26

Five women came from Christian backgrounds and yet, according to their narratives, at some point in their lives, they understood their need for the confession of personal faith in Jesus Christ as Lord and Savior (Servant-leaders #1, 3, 4, 5, 10). The other five were from different religious and other traditions and made a choice to believe and follow Jesus Christ (Servant-leaders #2, 6, 8, 9; one, Servant-leader #7, had no religious background).

All the women have had some sort of exposure to studying the Bible to varying intensities or degrees over different time periods. At least four women have had formal theological education, with Kim Cho earning her doctorate in recent years.

Despite the differences in their ages, each woman continues to serve in a ministry position in a Christian community and has undertaken theological or biblical studies at a significant point in her Christian lifetime; they have all engaged in informal, formal or non-formal Bible training during their Christian life growth period.

Testimony 1: Stepping into a Pastor's Shoes (South Korea)

Young Kim is a sixty-nine-year-old woman full of the warmth of Christ. She does not exhibit typical conservative Korean behavior: she lovingly hugs people. Korean women are usually culturally reserved, though they may greet a foreigner with a warm hug; among other Koreans, women of Young Kim's age will use a formal greeting. Young Kim lived in Japan in her younger and later years. She also lived in the United States when she and her husband relocated there for business reasons. Currently, she lives in South Korea but occasionally visits her children and grandchildren in Japan.

Though Young Kim's parents and grandparents were Christian, she responded to an altar call at one of the meetings of famous American evangelist Billy Graham in South Korea when she was fourteen years old.

She graduated with a pharmacy degree; after working for one year as a pharmacist, she married an ambitious non-Christian South Korean. They left for the USA two years after their marriage. Her husband carved out his career and established businesses in Hawaii and California. As a wife and mother, Young Kim understood her role was to follow her husband and raise their children – they had one child prior to their relocation to America and had another while in the USA. As a new mother Young Kim "could not do anything"; she was committed to being a mother and did not pursue her career.

However, in California her husband Samuel accepted Christ. His transformation was dramatic: as a family they attended church regularly, and Samuel conducted their Bible studies. He was more serious about God than Young Kim was at this stage. He did not tolerate any unbelief.

Samuel Kim became an outstanding pastor, missionary, visionary and a leader of a worldwide mission organization. He had a strong influence on her life after their marriage. Young Kim did not struggle too much with his character transformation but she did struggle with accepting her personal assurance of salvation. God worked on her value systems and she became more kingdom-minded.

Her husband was a strong leader, "pushing her down" as she came up, and she "just followed." She said, "When we started church in Japan, I did all the secretarial work. He only preached. I did all [other] things." Young Kim understood that she was not allowed to exercise any leadership. She was greatly influenced by the passion of her earthly role model (her husband Samuel) who modeled himself after Jesus in his passion to serve God till his last breath. Even after his death, his influence on her remains powerful. As Young Kim humbly said, "I wrote a book about Samuel's life." In the preface of her book, *The King's Invitation*, Young Kim writes: "Now my husband is sharing in His Master's happiness in Heaven. Once again, I resolve to run wholeheartedly in Samuel's blessed footsteps with the baton he handed to me."[1]

Her belief in her leadership skills was tested when she was asked to be the leader of the Japanese ministry in one of Korea's larger churches. This was the ministry founded by her husband when they returned to South Korea. She accepted the challenge. The baton has been handed to her. She has stepped into the pastor's shoes.

Young Kim now pastors members in this growing ministry but she is not an ordained pastor. She facilitates practical ministry courses, translates books from Korean into Japanese languages, and continues to be a loving grandmother to her grandchildren and a supportive mother to her children.

Testimony 2: Embracing the Precious Self in Christ (South Korea)

Despite being a polio victim at a young age, Kim Cho grew up comfortably in a family who encouraged her to be independent, strong and educated. Kim, fifty-six at the time of our interaction, has been a Christian for forty years. She

---

1. Kim, *King's Invitation*, 13.

accepted Christ as her Savior when she was in a South Korean high school. Though she comes from a family who practice Confucianism and Buddhism – the family's matriarch is a faithful Buddhist – Kim was released from any pressure to follow the family religion because of her status in the family: she is female and the youngest child. In Korean families, older children and especially sons are more important than younger girls.

Her Christian aunt, a professor at Euhwa University, and her aunt's good friend, an American missionary named Catherine, influenced her entry into Christian life. Kim was influenced by direct encounters with Catherine. Catherine's gentleness, kind smiles and joy in wartime Korea (1952) puzzled Kim.

Kim had her first experience of a worship service at Euhwa Women's High School, a Christian mission school. She played the piano for her friend who was singing at the school's Religious Emphasis Week dawn prayer meetings. A gospel meeting was held after the dawn prayer meetings and a pastor preached Jesus to all the students. At one meeting, Kim thought that it was strange that she should be considered "precious and not useless" by God, according to the sermon. Those words caused her to embark on a search for Jesus and, at sixteen years old, she gave her life to Jesus. Kim had discovered how precious she was to God.

In 1979, she furthered her studies and attended a church in the USA. Ten years after accepting Christ, she felt that she was not truly converted. Regular church attendance and a Bible study on the book of Romans did not convince her that she was converted to Christianity. Another ten years later, in 1989, she returned to South Korea as a wife and mother. Kim and her husband began teaching in South Korean institutions. They were busy parents with one son but they continued to attend church regularly.

In 1993, Kim and her husband Cho returned to the USA. This time, her husband was a visiting professor at a university in California. They continued to attend a Korean church in West Los Angeles for a year. One time, during the Evangelism Explosion course at church, she was asked the question, "If you died tonight, would you go to heaven?" She was sure she would go to heaven but was very, very embarrassed that she could not support her answer in great confidence. Her assurance of salvation was challenged and her response was so weak that she realized her folly – she had thought she was a Christian for more than twenty years. Her true conversion, according to Kim, was when she was thirty-six years old.

Kim had always been an optimistic person despite her physical disability. However, the realization of eternal life gave her "more reason to live in this world, not just for myself but for others." She began to look beyond herself. Prior to this true conversion, she was a self-disciplined and goal-oriented person for herself, but her conversion allowed her to extend these attitudes for the good of others.

Now aged fifty-six, Kim is a missionary with a heart for Muslim women. God has given her a gift of teaching. Her previous opportunities to teach piano lessons and musicology in various Korean colleges continue to be a foundation for her current teaching of the Bible and Christian life matters. She counsels other women and it is very "easy" for her to connect to the hearts of other people and empathize with their current difficult situations. Being able to speak scripturally into the lives of people in need of counsel makes her a leader of influence. At the time of our interaction, she had graduated with a doctor of philosophy degree and was in partnership with the Islamic Institute at Torch Trinity Graduate School of Theology in South Korea as a lecturer and researcher.

Testimony 3: Breaking Cultural Mindsets (India/Middle East)

Priscilla is an Indian based in the Middle East with her husband and two daughters. She became a Christian when she was thirteen years old at a fellowship meeting at her grandmother's home in India. At that time, she did not understand the gospel much but recognized that "Jesus is God and he is my Savior." Her family has a Christian background and Priscilla grew up reading the Bible, albeit as a ritual. As the only daughter, she had a good upbringing. Much later in life, she realized that her parents were not "born-again" Christians.

As a teenager growing up in India, she excelled in Sunday school preaching competitions but refused to be part of the youth fellowship as most members were "merry-makers." She was not interested in meaningless fun and concentrated on her studies. She married her husband when she was twenty-one years old, the customary age for young Indian ladies to get married. It was a blessing that her husband allowed her to complete her undergraduate degree in education after marriage. After the completion of her studies, she joined her husband in a very restricted Middle East nation.

In this nation, they had a daughter and Priscilla got a job as a teacher in a school. Still, both husband and wife sensed that they professed Christ but did not have a relationship with him. Since there was no church in this nation, they began attending an underground fellowship. This is where Priscilla's husband recommitted his life to Jesus.

Priscilla's recommitment to Christ came soon after, when she was twenty-four years old. Her husband had applied, prayed for and got a new job in another Middle Eastern nation. She, on the other hand, had great difficulty in getting a visa to join him. This family crisis directed her to turn to God for help. Priscilla finally got the visa and joined her husband in 1999 and they began to worship at an Indian church. She began to serve as a Sunday school teacher and, during the time of our interaction, was the headmistress of the Sunday school.

Priscilla and her husband began to hunger for discipleship and God brought systematic Bible training to them. I have had the pleasure of discipling and mentoring them for three years. Priscilla also serves as a facilitator with a mission organization and has discipled other leaders, some of whom are discipling others, too. She is also responsible for developing ministry in India with this organization. She spends a portion of her holiday period teaching in India. Her husband co-facilitates with her occasionally. Since 2010, Priscilla began cross-cultural discipleship beginning with fourteen Filipinos who committed their lives to Christ. She had to break her own cultural mindset about the abilities and capacities of Indian women in leadership before she could reach out to encourage others to rise up as servants of God.

Testimony 4: Standing Up for Christ (India/Middle East)

Ruth is a thirty-nine-year-old dentist who loves her work and her family, but most of all is passionate about exalting the name of Jesus. Ruth comes from a traditional Indian family that worships at a Syrian Orthodox church. Her childhood was spent in India but Ruth has also studied and worked in Middle Eastern nations. As a child, she understood church to be a place of prayer where people go to "ask God." Her parents taught her to "worship the saints and to do good works."

While she was studying in India, Ruth, who was then aged twelve, accepted Christ through her classmate's lifestyle evangelism and proclamation of the gospel. As a teenager, Ruth struggled with the idea of being a good Christian and this propelled her to read the Word rather randomly. Still, God spoke to her through her random reading, leading to her gradual transformation into Christlikeness.

When she was twenty years old, Ruth's faith in Christ was drastically challenged. She had a dream about her Muslim friend in college, and two days later, this Muslim girl accepted Christ. So Ruth and her friend would worship together, read the Word and attend all kinds of Christian meetings. When people got to know that a Muslim had become a Christian, the college was in commotion. The girls were threatened with expulsion, and another Muslim came to their room and removed the Bibles. When Ruth's Muslim-background Christian friend manifested the Holy Spirit's anointing, the school warden reported the matter to the dean, who promptly alleged that Ruth was calling on spirits. Earlier the school warden had questioned, "Who is leading here?" Ruth's response was, "The Holy Spirit is leading here." Muslim students banded together and encouraged others to sign a petition banning Ruth and three more students, who were also members of the church attended by Ruth, from talking about Jesus. An Islamic fundamentalist group threatened them with death. The dean issued them with a suspension from school, suspecting them of getting missionary support to carry out their evangelistic efforts. The latter allegation was denied by Ruth. Finally, the dean demanded that, if they wanted their suspension to be revoked, all four Christian students needed to sign a note stating that they would not speak of Jesus. Ruth and the other students stood up for Christ and refused to sign the note. Next, the dean demanded they sign if they wanted to pursue their education. Cornered in this way, the students had to sign a note, but the dean's intention backfired. Ruth remarked, "After this incident, many students came to us and told us that they wanted to follow us to church."

At age twenty-five, Ruth married a fellow dentist who worshipped at another traditional Indian church. Her husband had earlier accepted Christ as Lord and Savior at a fellowship meeting in a Middle Eastern nation.

Ruth had severe post-partum depression after her two children were born. While she doubted her ability to return to Christ after a period of moving away from God, God began to reveal himself through the Word. It was a time of direct training and understanding of God's righteousness. This period of "wilderness" would ultimately free her to a deeper understanding of being righteous in Jesus. By this time, the young family had relocated to another Middle Eastern nation.

On her first visit to a traditional church in this new location, she met Priscilla (see previous testimony) and sensed a kindred spirit. Priscilla began to disciple Ruth in a systematic Bible study program. Ruth successfully completed this study program and at the time of this interaction had begun to disciple others. In 2012, Ruth crossed cultures to teach a practical ministry course to Kenyans in Kenya.

Testimony 5: Serving Christ Till the Last Breath (Singapore)

The grand dame among the women in this book, Pushpamani, was eighty-six years old at the time of our interaction. Pushpamani, a Singaporean Indian, was originally born in Malaysia but had to leave the country when her Christian parents matched her with a Singaporean Christian Indian man who would become her husband. Her parents, especially her father, practiced the spiritual disciplines of prayer, reading the Bible and memorizing verses with his children. Pushpamani had ambitions to be a teacher or a missionary even before her marriage. Early in her marriage, Pushpamani became disappointed with the marriage, her husband and the general situation of her life. She realized that her husband was the exact opposite of her father. Her father had been a godly man with no vices, but she had married someone who gambled and "did not know how to live within his means." She even contemplated divorce, but her father disapproved and ordered her to stay with her husband. Divorce or being separated from a spouse is considered taboo in Indian culture.

She readily admitted that she truly became a Christian when she was forty-eight years old, almost twenty-three years after her marriage. She accepted Christ when she attended a course about the Holy Spirit at a church in Singapore. God slowly began to transform her, and her husband and children began to see this transformation. The fruit of this transformation was that the rest of the family began to attend church regularly and also became born-again Christians. At the time of our interaction, one of Pushpamani's sons was pursuing training to be a missionary.

Her courage and personal recognition of her spiritual gifts contributed to her confidence in Christ. She began to speak boldly about Jesus to others. Pushpamani's leadership experience began with teaching young people, but at the time of our interaction, she was leading and teaching a group of elderly women.

Note: Pushpamani went home to glory a few years after our interaction. She was a woman who loved people, and, in her eighties, would still speak about the Lord Jesus to anyone she knew. Her faith in Christ was strong, and she was the one who encouraged me to serve Holy Communion for the first time, to her and her husband when I visited their home. She was the Barnabas who gave me moral and prayer support to pursue my calling as a global missionary. Her desire was to speak of Jesus till her last breath, and this she did very well.

Testimony 6: A Second Chance for Godly Excellence (Singapore)

Lydia, sixty-three years old at the time of our interaction, has been married twice. She is a Singaporean Chinese woman who embraced Islam when she married her first husband, a Malaysian Muslim. During her first marriage, she lived in West Malaysia. She had married a wealthy man, was only twenty-five years old and was becoming a good Muslim; however, the couple separated after eight years of marriage and, soon after, Lydia stopped following Islamic ways. At this time, she also lost her first baby and their new house was still being renovated. It was a painful separation for Lydia.

Lydia took a step of faith and moved back to Singapore, connected with her Christian school friends and began to teach music. Her Christian friends wanted her to play the piano for them on a regular basis. Lydia played for four years at their meetings but still had not given her heart to Jesus.

It was an ultimatum issued by a prayerful friend that stirred Lydia to attend a Christian evangelistic rally. Her friend had told her that it would be Lydia's last chance to accept Christ and that she needed to attend the rally. By this time, Lydia had remarried and her husband accompanied her to the rally. Her husband was the person who introduced her to the Bible. At this rally in 1985, she surrendered to Jesus. God had given Lydia another chance to make it right with him. Soon after, Lydia, who had not wanted her first child, became pregnant and had a baby girl.

After her surrender to Jesus, Lydia was hungry for God's Word and God began to speak with her and teach her; she was beginning to understand the secret things of God. As her mind was renewed, she began to receive opportunities to serve God. She began serving in her first church's Sunday school, partly to keep an eye on her daughter. Then she moved on to another church and served in the Sunday school and later co-planted a church (with Kat – see next testimony). Over the years she continued to serve in this church plant as a teacher for the children and youth and as the head of various committees.

Lydia moved out of this church and now worships at a Baptist church in Singapore. She was invited to preach from the pulpit in 2013. She graduated from Bible school at age sixty-three and is teaching the Scriptures to other women. She has a heart of compassion and is very involved in ministry to the parents of children suffering from cancer. Lydia is now blessed to be a grandmother.

Testimony 7: Born to Lead (Singapore)

Kat is a doctor by profession and serves in a government clinic in Singapore. A Singaporean Chinese woman, she went to a Christian school and "grew up there." Her own family were more agnostic than Christian. Her parents married in a church but they were not Christians. Kat would later recognize the Creator God but she did not have a personal relationship with him; still, she thought she was a Christian. Her parents had no objections when Kat truly became a Christian at age sixteen.

A miracle occurred when she was sixteen. The school choir had travelled to West Malaysia to perform but Kat fell ill upon arrival. She was doubly upset because she fell sick on her birthday. Her belief that Christianity is literal and that she could take God at his word led her to pray. She sensed his presence in her room and, from her sixteenth birthday, understood that she would short-change herself if she ever walked away from God. She also experienced physical healing through this encounter with God.

Kat was not discipled but she "fed herself with the Word." She read voraciously on books related to Christian living. She went on to university and graduated with a medical degree. She married a fellow doctor and has two grown-up children. She is both mother and grandmother at this stage of her life.

Kat admitted that she desired to be a leader and believed that leadership was one of her spiritual gifts. Kat has more than fifteen years of church leadership experience. She has used her gift of teaching in care groups, youth groups and children's ministry, and has taught church leaders in various Asian nations. She has also co-planted a church (together with Lydia, see testimony above). Her husband partners with her and supports her growth as a leader and the ministries given to her. Kat was born to lead.

Testimony 8: Motherhood Is Leadership (Singapore)

Alice is the youngest among the ten women in this book. She is a Singaporean Chinese missionary who is married to an Australian missionary. They have three children and, as a family, were based in a Central Asian nation.[2] Alice has an undergraduate degree in Business and a postgraduate degree in Education and Intercultural Studies. The latter degree was earned at a Bible college where Alice and I were classmates. She is also a former pastor in a Presbyterian church in Singapore.

As a child, Alice lacked the love of her earthly father. She also worshipped Chinese gods. Alice trusted Jesus at a church youth camp when she was twelve years old. The camp preacher had shared about God's love and this attracted her to God. As a young adult, she had been part of the church's youth, church camp, and fund-raising and missions committees. Most importantly, she became recognized as a pastor in her church although she was not ordained. Soon after, she left for the mission field and met her husband within the first two years of serving in a restricted Central Asian nation.

At the time of our interaction, Alice was serving alongside her missionary husband mostly in a supporting role. Her time is occupied with household chores and caring for the children. Her husband has been instrumental in encouraging her to accept her leadership role as a mother. She confessed that she had "a difficult time accepting this idea," especially in comparison to a leadership role as pastor over a congregation. Alice has since accepted the concept that a mother is also a leader in ministry.

Testimony 9: Being Faithful to the Call of God (Malaysia)

Elizabeth's religious background stems from witchcraft and occultism. Her father encouraged his family to engage in occultism and traditional Iban practices which included offering animals and birds to the spirits. As an Iban in Sarawak, East Malaysia, this was a normal spiritual way of growing up in the longhouse. The Iban culture is a communal culture and, as recently as sixty years ago, Iban men were still headhunters. Elizabeth grew up in traditions that were steeped in paganism. An individualistic decision was not acceptable in an Iban family or community.

Elizabeth accepted Jesus during a church camp in 1978. However, she remained afraid to speak to her family about her conversion. She was then twenty-two years old. In later years, she would share the gospel and her whole

---

2. Alice and her family have since returned to Australia. They are ministering to mostly Asians within the vicinity of their residence.

family would come to know and commit their lives to Christ. Now in her sixties, Elizabeth has been an ordained pastor for the last three decades.

She has served with the Iban Methodist Church (Sarawak Iban Annual Conference) in various capacities – as chairperson of various church committees and as district superintendent. She was even responsible for overseeing the building of at least two of its largest churches.

When Elizabeth was in her late forties, she desired to further her undergraduate theological education. Male church leaders told her that she was too old to pursue further education but she insisted on God's plan for her. Subsequently, she crossed over to West Malaysia and studied at a theological seminary. She graduated with an undergraduate degree and teaches at a seminary in East Malaysia. She combines her pastoring and teaching gifts as she serves the seminary during the week and communities at the weekends. She continues to serve on various denominational committees.

Elizabeth said that, during the 1996 Methodist Women Annual conference, she shared her leadership experiences as one of the conference speakers: "I tried to encourage them on how God uses us and leads us. Some were encouraged, especially the young women. Being an Iban woman, it is hard to be a leader as Ibans are not open to women in leadership. In the longhouse, women are not allowed to speak, only the men . . . There are silent women who have the potential to be leaders. [We] need to encourage them; after training them, we must continue to follow up and encourage them. The men need to encourage the women. We work together. Sometimes, we need to give [a] chance to [the] men to join the women in leadership training. If they [the men] do not know what we are doing, they may think that we are doing better than them or doing something to challenge them."

This ordained pastor understood her imperfection and the depth of God's love for her when she accepted Christ as Lord and Savior. Elizabeth followed God's call as a pastor and has remained faithful. During her days as a new believer, other Christians had encouraged her. Thus, she continues to encourage others to be faithful to their call by God.

Testimony 10: Fulfilling the Call (Middle East)

RA had a difficult experience at four years of age. She was sent to a remote Catholic boarding school in Jordan. Her sister accompanied her. Their experiences at the boarding school were unpleasant and difficult. Powerless to voice her disagreement with being sent there, RA began to become resentful and angry with her parents. Her anger was especially directed towards her mother, who had not raised her voice to express her need to keep her children close to her. RA lacked parental love and blamed her mother for this insecurity. RA's father was then the distant breadwinner in the family as he worked in another Middle Eastern nation bordering the Persian Gulf.

When RA went to university to pursue a degree in journalism, she was ambitious and wanted "to be a celebrity journalist. This was all my dream and my thoughts revolved [around] being a successful journalist." While RA was at the university, a friend shared Campus Crusade's "Four Spiritual Laws" with her and she was astonished to hear that God loved her. The scriptural encounter during her friend's presentation of the "Four Spiritual Laws" impacted her enough to receive Christ. More importantly, RA had a sense of assurance that she was a child of God and was deeply loved by him. In time, she married a pastor and became a mother. Although RA's husband is pastor at a Baptist church, he has released his wife to grow for God. In 2010, RA graduated with a postgraduate degree in Women's Ministry.

RA's sense of deep unforgiveness towards her mother gnawed into her heart as God worked in her. As her understanding of God's love for her grew, she began to realize what would please him. She leaned on God to give her the strength to forgive her mother for being voiceless, and for not fighting to keep her children with her.

As RA grew in faith, she began to sense God's calling in her life. Her earthly ambitions were replaced by eternal prospects. She began her organization in 2000 and dedicated her life to equipping Arab women to reach and equip other Arab women. This organization begun by RA reaches Arab women in twenty-two Arab nations, fulfilling her call given by God.

Summary

The short narratives of each woman, including their salvation experiences, brief leadership development or growth and current ministries, supplement readers' knowledge about twenty-first-century Asian Christian women servant-leaders from various cultural and religious backgrounds. The ages of the women ranged from thirty-six to eighty-six years at the time of interacting with them. Only one woman in this group was an ordained pastor; another was a former pastor with no formal recognition. All of the women have had opportunities to pursue education goals. At least five women have postgraduate qualifications.

We will learn more about these women in the next chapters.

7

Christian Growth among Asian Christian Women Servant-Leaders According to the Narratives

E vangelical Christians are encouraged to look forward to a transformation that is dependent on internal changes. Believers in Christ are called to "walk in the same way" (1 John 2:6) as Jesus did, which is only possible if they abide in the one they believe in. The belief and abiding of Christians in Jesus Christ contributes to internal transformation that will affect the external environment with an eternal impact (Matt 5:13–16).

Key factors such as early growth environments – which include family backgrounds, educational environments and crisis experiences – encouragement from fellow Christians and other triggers that influenced the ten women's salvation and sanctification experiences form a true context for their movement into leadership experiences. There is an expected overlap between the sanctification process and leadership growth. In all of the narratives, Christian encouragers played an important part in their leadership growth process. We will learn more about these ten Asian Christian women servant-leaders from this chapter onwards.

Saving the Women

During our interactions, all of the women mentioned their family background and upbringing prior to accepting Christ. The women also mentioned their educational backgrounds. All of them have had some sort of biblical training in non-formal, informal or formal settings since they came to know Christ. It is interesting to note that not all of them attended Christian schools during their elementary and high-school days.

Ages of Asian Christian Women Leaders during Initial Salvation and Rededication

Regardless of whether she was born into a Christian family or not, each woman proceeded to commit her life to Christ totally[1] and personally, mostly after a better understanding of the basic doctrines.

Table 3 shows that five women (Servant-leaders #1–5) either had a rededication of their lives to Christ or true conversion experiences more than ten years after their initial acceptance of Christ. Young Kim depended on her parents' and grandparents' faith when she was younger. Her remark "My grandparents were Christians. My father's side were Christians" and her own later lack of understanding of her faith revealed that her knowledge of salvation by faith was initially minimal. Later in Young Kim's life, and especially after her marriage, she would question herself regarding her personal salvation until God reminded her of Hebrews 6:10: "For God is not unjust so as to overlook your work and the love that you have shown for his name in serving the saints, as you still do."

Only Pushpamani (Servant-leader #5) said that she grew up observing Christian disciplines (such as praying as a family, memorizing Bible verses, reading the Word and going to church). Yet she had a true conversion when she was forty-eight years old after she understood from God's Word the requirements for salvation.

---

1. Each woman knew that she could not turn back on Christ; she had willingly chosen to follow this path of righteousness and her entire being belonged to Christ alone.

Table 3: Ages of Asian Christian Women Leaders

Interviewee No:	Name / Current Age	Age at Initial Salvation	Reason for Initial Salvation	Age at (rd) or (tc)	Reason for (rd) or (tc)*
1	Young Kim / 69	14	Emotional / Volitional	30	Quiet faith in understanding through God's Word that God knows her (rd)
2	Kim Cho / 58	16	Being precious in God's eyes	36	Understanding through God's Word of salvation by faith (tc)
3	Priscilla / 39	13	Intellectual / Volitional	24	Faithfulness of God through experience (rd)
4	Ruth / 39	12	Intellectual / Volitional	27	Does not specify but it is a rededication
5	Pushpamani / 86	As a child	Not Applicable (N/A)	48	God's Word (tc)
6	Lydia / 62	26	Surrender to God	N/A	N/A
7	Kat / 54	16	Faithfulness of God through experience	N/A	N/A
8	Alice / 36	12	God's personal love	N/A	N/A
9	Elizabeth / 61	22	Eternal life	N/A	N/A
10	RA / 44	19	God's personal love and need for a relationship with God	N/A	N/A

* "rd" refers to rededication of self to Christ while "tc" refers to true conversion to Christ

The other five interviewees (Servant-leaders #6–10) made a total commitment to God during their initial decision and they never wavered in their faith. Alice and RA (Servant-leaders #8 and 10) were especially in need of God's personal love for them. For example, RA responded as follows to her Arab Christian friend who was trying to evangelize her: "What do you mean [when you say that] God loves me and has a better plan for me? I have been suffering [since] my childhood; my parents put me in a dormitory. So what kind of better plan is there?" When RA accepted Christ for the first time after a thorough explanation of the gospel, she conceded, "[I] need a relationship with him [Jesus]."

Family backgrounds and upbringings, regardless of their positive or negative impact, played an important part in the Asian Christian women servant-leaders' salvation experiences. The rededication or true conversion experiences were mostly due to a better understanding of God's Word and an assurance of their faith in Christ.

Family Background/Upbringing Influences Transformation

Negative parental influences are parental influences upon their children without Christ as a focus. The parents may be unbelievers or believers who lack an understanding of biblical values and do not live transformed lives. Negative past circumstances refers to the environment or situation without Christ that was encountered by the Asian Christian women servant-leaders in their Christian life journey. Sometimes, they had to make a conscious personal shift away from their birth family's lack of understanding and/or false beliefs about Christianity or other religions, in the direction of true Christian beliefs.

One of them, Elizabeth, said, "I had Iban beliefs – beliefs in evil spirits [and in] many gods like trees, snakes, animals, and ghosts for more than twenty years. My father was a witch doctor and he was strict about observing these beliefs." Before she became a Christian, they would have family worship at midnight and would make offerings to their gods. Every family member had to participate by wearing the Iban dress and offer to the gods. Elizabeth experienced negative influences and circumstances.

RA was a Catholic and was "forced to go to church, forced to fast, forced to follow Jesus, forced to pray to Mary." This was a negative circumstance that RA experienced, but, at nineteen years of age, she accepted Jesus Christ while at university. RA saw her need for a relationship with Christ. She understood that this time, she was free to make a choice. She said that she knew that she loved the Lord Jesus. Her desire to be a good person is now born out of choice and the love of God in her, and not out of self-strength.

Ruth was born into a traditional Orthodox Christian family who believed that they had direct blessings from the Syrian Antioch churches and were proud of being the original Christians. Ruth states, "My dad said that his family came from the direct line of the first few people who believed the message given by the apostle Thomas [one of the Lord's disciples] when he [the apostle Thomas] came to India. The first believers were Brahmins[2] before and they accepted Jesus by faith at that time. My parents used to go to Velangani.[3] She [Mary] is supposed to have appeared there. We used to go to Parumala Thirumeni,[4] another saint in Kerala. I somehow knew that he [the Lord Jesus Christ] was the answer to all the questions in my heart." Ruth experienced both positive and negative parental influences in her early growth as a Christian. For example, she had well-meaning and prayerful parents who cared about her personal growth as a person. She was encouraged to pursue higher education and become a dentist. However, her parents' worship of idols coupled with attendance at their church confused Ruth. This was a negative influence that stunted her growth as a Christian. Nevertheless, her testimony reveals that she sought other Christians whose lives seemed to be "different."

Table 4 provides a summary of family backgrounds that contributed to the women's spiritual formation.

Table 4: Early Growth Environments: Family Background/Upbringing

Elements	Family Background / Upbringing
(1) Negative parental influences and past circumstances that affected spiritual growth in a positive manner	9
From non-Christian homes (a)	6
From Christian homes (a)	3
(2) Positive parental influences and past circumstances that contributed to spiritual growth	5
From non-Christian homes (b)	2
From Christian homes (b)	3

2. Brahmins are the highest caste in the Hindu caste system and most were from the priestly order.

3. Velangani is a Catholic church where people worship Jesus's mother Mary.

4. Parumala Thirumeni is highly revered by the Orthodox Syrian Church in India. Information about Parumala Thirumeni can be found at http://parumalathirumeni.org/.

Nine Asian Christian servant-leaders had to deal with ungodly influences and/or past circumstances and overcame them with godly transformation of their mindsets and hearts. Six of them came from animistic, agnostic, Buddhist, Chinese religion or Islamic backgrounds. The other three women, despite their Christian backgrounds, did not have positive influences in their life journey. An understanding of biblical truths helped all of them to make conscious paradigm shifts.

From an evangelical Christian perspective, the background of eighty-six-year-old Pushpamani is an example of a good and positive Christian upbringing. She had a consistent spiritual upbringing at home – studying the Bible and memorizing verses, praying and worshipping God, and obeying her parents. However, her life journey did not always continue in this positive manner. Her testimony revealed that she struggled in later years to love her husband who prevented her from going to church. The circumstances of her becoming a mother and wife too quickly were personally negative experiences. Yet she overcame these circumstances through her positive upbringing in the Word and her own faith in the Word.

Another example is Alice, who came from a Chinese religious background. Her mother was involved in Chinese religious practices. These were negative influences, but Alice was, with her mother's permission, able to attend Sunday school at a church, which was a positive influence and circumstance. Her mother's permission would pave the way for Alice to accept Christ at a church youth camp at the age of twelve.

Positive parental influences refers to bringing up children in a wholesome manner regardless of whether the parents are professing Christians, nominal Christians or non-believers. For Christian parents, positive parental influence would include bringing up children in a biblically sound manner through prayer, attending church, and allowing them to participate in fellowships that enhance their living for God. Positive past circumstances refers to environments or situations which allowed the Asian Christian women servant-leaders to continue their personal and Christian spiritual growth without any adverse effects on their physical or psychological states.

Kat's agnostic parents were encouraging and she did not experience many difficulties at home. It was an easy and smooth life for her. She had freedom in making life choices. There were no serious objections from her parents or even tense relationships at home when she decided to attend a church or become a Christian. However, for Kat to mature as a Christian, she endured tests of faith with a clear understanding of the power in God's Word.

It is notable that the women who experienced negative parental influences or negative circumstances in their lives matured into Christlikeness once they had an understanding of deep forgiveness and healing of their being. Those who had some positive parental influences and/or past circumstances went through crisis experiences and struggles during the journey to be more like Christ. Our humble response to God in any kind of circumstance is dependent on our entrenchment in biblical truths.

Christian Activities as Open Doors for Spiritual Growth

Church and Christian activities such as youth camps, religious emphasis weeks, and worship and prayer services in Christian schools were influential in the women's lives as they learned about and grew in their Christian faith.

Alice was invited to a youth camp where the pastor shared about God's love and "all the evidences that there is a God who loves me and died for me" (Alice). Pushpamani attended a course on the baptism of the Holy Spirit at a church and started reading the Word thereafter.

Table 5 provides a summary of the main Christian activities that introduced the women to the invitation to place their faith in Christ. Christian school-based events, fellowships and Bible studies were the activities that contributed to the initial learning and growing process of the ten Asian Christian women servant-leaders.

Table 5: Activities Influencing the Introduction and Growth in Christian Faith

Activities	Introduction to Christian Faith
Church fellowship	9
Bible study groups	7
Christian school-based events*	2
Personal evangelism	2
Spiritual disciplines at home	1

* All Christian schools have an affiliation with a church, denomination or mission agency.

Nine of the women were introduced to the Christian faith through church fellowships that included such things as youth camps, home groups, prayer meetings or other events organized by the church. Pushpamani was involved in church activities such as the women's fellowship, prayer meetings and Bible studies. These activities strengthened her faith. She was also the only person in this group who had practiced strong and positive spiritual disciplines at home from an early age. In Lydia's case, she was an unbeliever when she got involved in a Christian home group as a pianist. Her constant participation in the home group as a pianist eventually increased her understanding of Christian love and faith, such that she accepted Christ as Lord and Savior. Lydia also experienced Christian faith acting in Christian love when, soon after her conversion, she was hospitalized following a spiritual attack on her. Her Christian friends' love and care through prayer and daily visits during her hospitalization helped her considerably to overcome this difficult experience in her life.

The Christian journeys for seven of the women were influenced by regular Bible studies. Priscilla's faith grew as she met with others to study the Bible. Priscilla not only studied the Bible but also allowed the Holy Spirit to guide her into obedience. As she did this, she began to be more and more involved in God's work.

Kim Cho experienced her first steps of transformation through a school-based activity. Since she was a good pianist, she was asked to play the piano during a religious emphasis week, even though she was not a believer. During that week, she gave her life to Jesus. Another woman, Kat, experienced God's presence during a school outing, at which point she knew that God was with her. This encounter with God became a turning point in Kat's life.

As new believers who had accepted Jesus into their lives, the women felt a need to connect immediately with other believers through Bible studies or home groups and attend group events held by their churches. Lydia was the only one who was welcomed into a ministry before she accepted Christ. Fellowship for the purpose of edification and growing together in the Word was important to all of them. God does work in mysterious ways. We Christians are often ready to put God in a box, such that when something "unusual" happens, we are mentally paralyzed and unable to fathom his goodness and greatness.

Growing as Christ-Centered Women

Our sanctification in Christ starts as soon as we have accepted the Lord Jesus Christ. We are "predestined to be conformed to the image of his Son" (Rom 8:29). When I accepted Christ at the age of thirteen at a school chapel service, I never understood that Christ had to be Lord. The message of forgiveness portrayed Christ as Savior, but not as both Lord and Savior. I definitely doubted my own salvation. Thankfully, I was rescued from my ignorance eighteen years later when I was disciplined by a church leader. My life was put on the fast track once I determined in my mind and heart that no other can be Lord and Savior except Jesus Christ of Nazareth.

Similarly, in the narratives, five women doubted their initial salvation commitment. They therefore recommitted their lives to Christ at a later time. Christians comprising mentors, role models and encouragers influenced the women servant-leaders at different leadership growth phases, over a period of time.

Spiritual Influences

Life experiences such as marriage, divorce, unforgiveness towards a parent or sickness caused some of the women to make decisions that had consequences that impacted themselves directly and others indirectly. These life experiences were a part of their ongoing sanctification towards Christlikeness.

Alice was not prepared for marriage. It was an arranged marriage and she had no choice but to honor her parents and accept it. After she met Christ, her attitude changed and she believed that she could overcome the challenges of marriage with God's help.

RA showed her relief when she shared, "God started working on my heart. I lived for many days in anger and resentment – this is not what God wants for his children. I forgave my mother. I take care of her now."

Kat started to read the Bible in a new way. She confessed that she "took it like the Yellow Pages. I saw everything in there as something that I could have. I could not understand why Christianity needed to be anemic."

Table 6 summarizes the key influences that motivated the Asian Christian women servant-leaders to transform in Christ and the results of their transformation at certain points in their lives.

Three factors affected the transformation of the ten Asian Christian women leaders after their initial salvation. They were not immediately discipled and engaged in God's Word by themselves with the help of the Holy Spirit.

Eight women mentioned that understanding God's Word clearly allowed them to make various changes and decisions. These women were assured of their salvation, acquired a vision to reach others, adopted godly attitudes and desires, became committed to God, became confident in Christ, and understood that past cultural-religious practices that did not please God must be ended. For example, Ruth's understanding of some basic Christian teaching allowed her to question her parents' worship of the saints, while Priscilla realized that she should not continue wearing the *bindi*, which is the red dot worn on the forehead by Hindu women. Elizabeth "left the [Iban] traditions [that displease God]" when she accepted Christ.

Table 6: Factors Affecting Transformation and Consequences after Initial Salvation

Factors (N)*	Consequences	Impact
Understanding God's Word (8)	1. Assurance of salvation 2. Acquired vision to reach others 3. Change in attitudes and desires – selfishness turning to godliness 4. Commitment to God 5. Confidence in Christ 6. Understanding that past cultural-religious practices displeased God and ending such practices	Self Family
Recognition and acceptance of the personal love and faithfulness of God (5)	1. Confidence in Christ 2. Purpose in life 3. Able to forgive self and others 4. Able to overcome depression 5. Able to persevere through persecution 6. Seeking and desiring God more	Self Family Others
Spiritual encounters (2) (a) Presence of the Holy Spirit (b) Demonic oppression	1. Surrender of self to God 2. Deliverance	Self

*   Where (N) is the number of citations by the women.

Half the group mentioned personally recognizing and accepting God's love and faithfulness. This recognition and acceptance established an intimate relationship with God. They became more confident, knew their purpose, and were able to extend forgiveness to others, overcome depression and persevere through persecutions. These women were motivated to seek and desire a deeper intimacy with God. For instance, Ruth experienced God's faithfulness as she persevered through two persecutions in her early Christian life. The first persecution happened when her parents beat her for questioning their worship of the saints. The second persecution occurred when she was locked up in her room at the college and threatened with expulsion because the school staff and Muslim students thought she had influenced a young Muslim girl to convert to Christ.

Lydia especially surrendered to God when she sensed his presence at an evangelistic rally. In addition, she was also healed and delivered from demonic oppression and moved forward in Christian living.

Christian Encouragers

All of the Asian Christian women servant-leaders have had encouragement to pursue ministry leadership from one or more persons in their lives. Christians have influenced them through their role modeling of Christian beliefs, spiritual disciplines and behavior. The gender of such encouragers was not restricted to female. In other words, even male Christians had been used by God to influence the lives of some of these Asian Christian women servant-leaders.

Singaporean Indian Pushpamani started with the Women's Society of Christian Service (WSCS) in her Methodist church. "Mrs Tan Beng Leong (a Singaporean Christian Chinese leader) used to encourage me. She was [a] mentor to me. She encouraged me in [my] spiritual life and led me in prayer," said Pushpamani.

Priscilla mentioned an elderly professor, Abraham Mathew, who was her mentor and role model and a Sunday school teacher. Priscilla loved to hear him preach and declared that "he really made me understand about salvation and judgment."

Table 7 summarizes the means of encouragement given by Christian encouragers to the women.

Mentors

Only one Indian woman experienced mentorship under a male professor who was also a teacher-preacher at the traditional Indian church. Priscilla, with the blessing of her husband, studied the Bible with this mentor. The mentor saw her potential and asked her to teach the church's Sunday school. She still remembers his words given at a Vacation Bible School (VBS) meeting to all the teachers more than a decade ago: "You are accountable for what you do for the VBS. If you have been entrusted with the beginner class, you might be thinking [of] telling some stories, let the children color some pictures and then go home. But on that day when you stand before the Lord, he will be interested to know if you did what was entrusted to you [faithfully]."

Table 7: Encouragers of Asian Christian Women Servant-Leaders

Encouragers (Number of women who cited them)	Categories of Relationship to Women (Number)	Means of Encouragement (Number of citations)
Mentors: (a) Male (1)	Bi-vocational missionary (1)	Teaching Bible accurately (1), prayer and moral support (1), invitation to minister alongside (1), accountability (1)
(b) Female (3)	School teachers (3), friend (1), cross-cultural missionary (1), pastor (1)	Teaching Bible accurately (2), prayer and moral support (5), invitation to minister alongside (1), accountability (1)
Motivators: (a) Male (9)	Christian spouses (7), pastors (4), Christian children (1)	Spousal blessing for them to be leaders in Christian ministry (7), pursuit of further theological education (2), pursuit of excellence (1), pursuit of ministry activities (1)
(b) Female (4)	Friends (2), Christian children (2)	Mutual encouragement (3), prayer support (3)
Role model: (a) Male (1)	Bi-vocational missionary (1)	Preaching accurately (1)
(b) Female (2)	Cross-cultural missionary (2)	Joy during war time (1), showing that women can carry out many types of service for God (1)

Female schoolteachers of three women (Ruth, Alice and Kat) were important mentors. They mostly offered spiritual encouragement through prayer, counseling and the occasional explanation of questions related to the Bible and life situations. A theologically trained pastor and a cross-cultural missionary also ministered with accurate Bible teaching to Alice and Priscilla respectively.

Motivators

Out of the nine married women, seven were blessed and encouraged to move ahead in Christian leadership by their spouses. Two women, one a Korean and the other a Singaporean Indian, did not have the support of their husbands to be active in ministry until much later in their lives. According to her narrative, Young Kim became active as a ministry leader after her husband's death, while Pushpamani became active in ministry after her husband accepted Christ and her children had grown up. Pushpamani, however, had the encouragement of her children – they released her to be involved in church ministry, essential in her leadership growth. Male pastors played an important role in encouraging two women (Young Kim and Elizabeth) to pursue excellence.

Female friends and daughters were instrumental in encouraging the women with mutual sharing and prayer support.

Role Models

Only one interviewee, Priscilla, had a male role model. He was a professor in a restricted nation and also taught and preached in one of the traditional Indian churches. This mentor exhibited godly character and respect for emerging leaders. His accurate preaching of the Word impressed Priscilla.

Cross-cultural missionaries were role models for both Priscilla and Kim Cho. For example, the behavior of an American cross-cultural missionary who was always smiling despite the difficult conditions of the Korean War in 1952 was a seed in young Kim Cho's mind and heart. The fear, hardship and painful sufferings of war contrasted with the friendly and warm personality of the foreign missionary and planted a seed of curiosity. Later on, Kim Cho discovered that Jesus was the reason for the American missionary's joy and ended up becoming a missionary herself. As for Priscilla, who came from a traditional Indian church context which did not allow women to exercise leadership, she was impacted by a Singaporean Indian cross-cultural missionary (me). Her eyes were opened to the possibilities of ministry as a woman servant-leader when she met me. Priscilla saw that I did "many things."[5] In Priscilla's mind, these possibilities were reachable.

Discussion

A discussion of the narratives reveals a category of people ready for the gospel, the need for clear proclamation and persuasion of the gospel to those at a vulnerable young age, and the importance of having believers engage with activities initiated by the church or Christians. It also reveals an understanding of key encouragers in the process of sanctification.

Need for Clarity in Gospel Communication and Assurance of Salvation

Most of the women sought to identify themselves with Christ at a young age due to various influences. Unfortunately, not all received a clear gospel message. Their identity was insecure in Christ. This caused half the group to rededicate themselves or have a true conversion at a later age.

In terms of culture, Confucianism affects South Koreans and Singaporean Chinese people. Yet the responses to the gospel among the Singaporean Chinese women were firm while the South Korean women doubted their salvation. All of these women came from non-Christian backgrounds that were culturally influenced by Confucianism. The Singaporean Chinese women's firm responses were a result of the clear communication of the gospel by those serving in the role of evangelists and preachers, and a clear understanding of the gospel by those hearing it. Clarity in gospel communication and assurance of salvation would certainly help Asian women to be rooted firmly in their Christian beliefs from the first day of accepting Christ as Lord and Savior (initial salvation).

---

5. I have discipled and mentored Priscilla for six years (2005–2011). In the second half of this period, Priscilla became my co-worker on my team in my previous mission organization. In those six years, Priscilla observed how I pioneered new ministries, headed global operations, evangelized, and readily engaged in healing, prophetic, teaching and preaching ministries. She also knew that I spent much time seeking God and being in his perfect will, and was doing doctoral studies with Tabor Adelaide. She has observed my ready relocations to four different nations within a span of six years and knows of my friendship and discipleship across varied culture groups.

Wholesome Discipleship for Asian Christian Women

Asian Christian women are uniquely placed amidst various cultural and religious environments. Some are placed in nations that restrict the gospel or are hostile to it. Most Asian Christian women carry ungodly practices and past emotional and spiritual hurts and wounds as they step into a relationship with Christ. None of the ten women in this book was discipled after receiving Christ. This resulted in them trying to wrestle with and understand God's Word by themselves. Wholesome discipleship would be beneficial for Asian Christian women who have just accepted Christ. Spiritual encounters are a reality in Asia and therefore ministry in the power of the Holy Spirit subjected to the truth of God's Word has the potential to move these women at a quicker pace. The manifestation of God's love and faithfulness in the lives of these women was a strong factor in their transformation, but stronger than that manifestation is the understanding of God's Word.

Godly Encouragers

Current and emerging women servant-leaders need godly encouragers. Pastors play a crucial role in identifying emerging leaders and guiding them into further education – theological or professional. Every married woman who is a servant-leader needed the blessing of her husband; this blessing is both the "male covering" required by complementarians and respect required by egalitarians. Single women, like the ordained pastor, Elizabeth, need encouragement from both pastors and fellow Christian brothers and sisters.

Men were the majority motivators according to the narratives. The mentors and role models for these Asian Christian women servant-leaders were primarily other women. However, from my personal experience and observation of other women, this is not necessarily the case for all Asian women. In my own life, male leaders within the Christian environment were my primary motivators and mentors for more than two decades. I have had only one female mentor for a period of three years.

Opening Wide the Doors for Non-Christians and Christians

Most Asians are communal by nature and therefore it is perfectly acceptable to have non-Christians helping out at fellowships, school meetings and church events. Asian women from mostly patriarchal nations need to have a sense of belonging to someone or to some group.

Asian women at a young age are seeking not only their identity but also love and trust. Guided seeking with the church's help allowed these ten women to place their trust in Jesus. Ruth stated that she had always thought church was a place for prayers. Asian churches, except some in South Korea, do not have an open-door policy for anyone to walk into the sanctuary and pray or receive prayer. Increasing security issues and restrictions at worship venues will pose a challenge to both the church and those who wish to pray. An open-church concept would be an option for further exploration in countries receptive to the gospel.

The mobilization of Asian Christian women servant-leaders is dependent on their knowledge of the Word, their experience with God and their obedience in fulfilling God's mission. Group Bible study brought most of these women to the saving and living knowledge of God. Some were engaged in Bible study even before they became believers. Here is an indication that cell or care groups need not be exclusive to Christians. This is another example of the need to open the doors wide to reach other Asian women.

Summary

The road to salvation and sanctification is long and narrow. The cultural, religious and educational environments of these ten Asian Christian women servant-leaders were significant in molding their personal identities. Parental influences in the cultural contexts of the Asian Christian women leaders were both positive and negative. Non-believers or seekers of God were blessed to use their talents in Christian groups. These women had a hunger to engage with God's Word. The experiences of God's love and faithfulness and spiritual encounters were causal factors in the process of sanctification.

As these ten Asian Christian women servant-leaders grew in and with Christ, they began to learn from Christian encouragers – mentors, motivators and role models. These were the people whom God sent at different times of their Christian life journey. Spousal blessing for women to minister as servant-leaders was strongly indicated in their narratives.

8

Call to Serve by Leading According to the Narratives

The evangelical Christian perspective on Christian life and leadership determines that the understanding of Scripture demands a faith-based, obedient response to fulfill God's plans. Clinton calls this the ministry-maturing phase where "God challenges the leader into ministry."[1] Here, each Asian Christian woman servant-leader describes her call to leadership ministry and development for leadership in the Christian community.

Obeying the Call to Leadership

God uses a variety of methods to draw people to himself; similarly, leaders receive their call to ministry in creative ways. There may have been other influences and even other people who were instrumental in encouraging, challenging and allowing these ten Asian Christian women servant-leaders to blossom into leadership. However, although this information is limited in that it is strictly drawn from the narratives, it does give a reasonable overview of the leadership journey taken by them.

To identify the main calls of the women as expressed through their narratives I used a passage from Ephesians, as well as definitions based on biblical evidence, observations, and Clinton and Clinton's reasoning in *Unlocking Your Giftedness.*[2]

Most evangelical Christians would agree that disciples of Christ continue to function in the offices or at least operate the gifts described in Ephesians

---

1. Clinton, *The Making*, 67.
2. Clinton and Clinton, *Unlocking Your Giftedness*, 142–147.

4:11–12. It is also possible for Christian leaders to operate in other functions to fulfill their call and therefore it is possible for leaders to be multigifted.[3]

> And he gave the apostles,[4] the prophets,[5] the evangelists,[6] the shepherds [pastors][7] and teachers,[8] to equip the saints for the work of ministry, for building up the body of Christ. (Eph 4:11–12)

In Table 8, I assigned and prioritized three gifts based on a combination of factors: the interviewees' descriptions of their responsibilities in their narratives, their self-identification of their call during the interviews and my personal observation of each woman (except RA) as we engaged in ministry together. For example, Young Kim's call is "pastor/teacher/apostle": this indicates that while she is a missionary (apostle) and teaches leaders, her primary calling is that of a pastor, as it was evident in her life narrative. Table 8 also identifies the women's call to leadership at different points in time, how they were developed and the types of opportunities that were available to them. The call of each woman was listed in order of priority.

I used the abbreviations "cd," "md," "pd" and "sd" as abbreviations for character development, mental development, physical development and spiritual development respectively.

---

3. Clinton and Clinton, 146.

4. Apostles create new ministries, as seen in the lives of various New Testament disciples like the original eleven, Paul, Timothy, Titus and others. The person possesses a "spiritual leadership capacity to move with authority from God to create new ministry structures . . . Traditionally, apostolic gift has been associated with missionary work because the pioneering work was easy to see" (Clinton and Clinton, 145). The authors add that not all missionaries possess this gift.

5. Prophets deliver predictive truth or situational truth from God publicly in order to exhort, edify, counsel or convince others of the truth. The prophet speaks with authority and conviction from God and exposes the will of God (Clinton and Clinton, 144).

6. Evangelists persuade others to accept Christ as their Lord and Savior. They are concerned for lost souls and communicate with authority from God to influence others to accept the way of the kingdom (Clinton and Clinton, 147).

7. Pastors care for and encourage their church members to grow into Christlikeness through modeling, protecting them from error and disseminating the truth. Qualifications are listed in 1 Tim 3 and Titus 1. There are many Christians who operate as a pastor without holding the office of the pastor (Clinton and Clinton, 146).

8. The gift of teaching is mentioned in three major New Testament passages (1 Cor 12; Rom 12; Eph 4). The teacher is described as someone with the ability to "instruct, explain and expose Biblical truth" in such a way that others are able to understand the truth (Clinton and Clinton, 142).

Table 8: Call, Development and Opportunities for Asian Christian Women Servant-Leaders According to the Narratives

Name	Type of Call According to Eph 4:11–12	Key Leadership Development / Type of Development	Key Opportunities, Scope and Age Frame
Young Kim	Pastor/Teacher/Apostle	1. Assurance of salvation (sd) 2. Submission (cd) 3. Honing of skills (pd)	1. Student leader (local) (youth) 2. Secretary to pastor of Japanese church plant in Japan (international) (adult) 3. Facilitator of courses for church leaders (local and international) (adult) 4. Unordained pastor of Japanese ministry in South Korea (local) (adult) 5. Author (local) (adult) 6. Mother and grandmother (family) (adult)
Kim Cho	Teacher/Pastor/Apostle	1. True conversion to Christ (sd) 2. Increased faith (sd) 3. Compassion (cd)	1. Music teacher (local) (adult) 2. Facilitator of courses for church leaders (local and international) (adult) 3. Counselor (local) (adult) 4. Lecturer (local) (adult) 5. Senior researcher (local) (adult) 6. Mother (family) (adult)

Name	Type of Call According to Eph 4:11–12	Key Leadership Development / Type of Development	Key Opportunities, Scope and Age Frame
Priscilla	Teacher/Pastor	1. Renewal of faith (sd) 2. Honing of skills (pd) 3. Mentored into leadership (md, sd) 4. Mindset change to understand that women can serve God in many ways (md) 5. Desire to serve God (cd, sd)	1. Schoolteacher (international) (youth) 2. Sunday school teacher (local) (young adult) 3. Facilitator of courses for church leaders (local & regional) (adult) 4. Tutor (international) (adult) 5. Coordinator for ministry (local) (adult) 6. Founding member of fellowship in a restricted nation (local) (adult) 7. Mother (family) (young adult) 8. Tutor (local) (adult)
Ruth	Pastor/Teacher	1. Understanding of basic doctrine (md) 2. Increased faith (sd) 3. Mentoring into leadership (md, sd)	1. Sunday school teacher (local) (adult) 2. Facilitator of courses for church leaders (local & regional) (adult) 3. Founding member of fellowship in a restricted nation (regional) (adult) 4. Mother (family) (adult) 5. Dentist (local) (adult)
Push-pamani	Teacher/Evangelist	1. True conversion to Christ (sd) 2. Mentoring into leadership (md, sd) 3. Desire to serve God (cd, sd)	1. Sunday school teacher (local) (adult) 2. Prayer leader (local) (adult) 3. Care group leader (local) (adult) 4. Mother and grandmother (family) (adult)

Name	Type of Call According to Eph 4:11–12	Key Leadership Development / Type of Development	Key Opportunities, Scope and Age Frame
Lydia	Pastor/Teacher	1. Acceptance of service as a non-Christian in a Christian care group (md) 2. Surrender to God's will (sd) 3. Willingness to step into new service (cd, sd)	1. Sunday school teacher (local) (adult) 2. Nurse (local) (young adult) 3. Founding member of church plant in Singapore (local) (adult) 4. Chairperson of various church committees (local) (adult) 5. Care group leader (local) (adult) 6. Bible teacher (local) (adult) 7. Mother (family) (adult)
Kat	Teacher/Prophetess	1. Acknowledging deception in life (md, sd) 2. Accepting God literally for his Word (md, sd) 3. Guided by a mentor into spiritual truth (md, sd) 4. Inner knowledge that leadership is her personal gift from God (sd) 5. Desire to serve God (cd, sd)	1. Sunday school teacher (local) (adult) 2. Founding member of church plant in Singapore (local) (adult) 3. Chairperson of various church committees (local) (adult) 4. Care group leader (local) (adult) 5. Bible teacher (local and international) (adult) 6. Mother (family) (adult) 7. Doctor (local) (adult)

Name	Type of Call According to Eph 4:11–12	Key Leadership Development / Type of Development	Key Opportunities, Scope and Age Frame
Alice	Pastor/Teacher/Apostle	1. Accepting the personal love of God (md, sd) 2. Conversion to Christ (sd) 3. Strong desire to participate in church activities (cd, sd) 4. Self-consideration as a leader because she is a mother (md)	1. Pastor (local) (young adult) 2. Cross-cultural missionary (regional) (young adult) 3. Mother (Family) (adult)
Elizabeth	Pastor/Teacher	1. In-family opportunity to care for younger siblings (cd) 2. Conversion to Christ (sd) 3. Self-confidence in Christ (cd, sd) 4. Mentoring into ministry (md, sd) 5. Audible voice of God questioning her future direction (sd) 6. Recognition of leadership gift in self (cd, md, sd) 7. Willingness to be a leader since childhood (cd, sd)	1. Older sister (family) (child) 2. Youth leader (local) (adolescence) 3. Sunday school teacher (local) (young adult) 4. Student leader in theological school (local) (adult) 5. Ordained pastor (local) (young adult) 6. District superintendent (local) (adult) 7. Seminary teacher (local) (adult)
RA	Apostle/Pastor/Teacher	1. Acceptance of the personal love of God (md, sd) 2. Conversion to Christ (sd) 3. Transformation to kingdom mind and heart (cd, md, sd) 4. Understanding of the call (md)	1. Founder of non-profit organization (regional) (young adult) 2. Mother (family) (young adult)

Call

As the women processed their salvation, sanctification or transformation experiences, the natural next step was to enter the Lord's service. The narratives indicate that the women servant-leaders' primary calls are those of a pastor and/ or teacher and/or apostle. Yet among the women, only one woman currently serves as an ordained pastor, while another is a former pastor who continues to pastor her children. Even though four women were identified as apostles (missionaries), only one woman had a significant calling as an apostle as she pioneered a new ministry.

A majority of the Asian Christian women servant-leaders had the pastor-teacher or teacher-pastor calling. This is significant information that affirms the pastoral-teaching gifts of Asian Christian women servant-leaders.

Leadership Development

The first steps of all ten women on their leadership journey began with one or more of these process events: a true conversion, an assurance of salvation, understanding of God's attribute and teachings, and a surrender to God's will. This led to an increase in faith or a renewal of faith. Most of the leadership development discussion overlaps with the previous chapter's discussion of the various influences affecting the salvation and sanctification processes. All of the Asian Christian women servant-leaders generally had good and calm personalities; they did not have a disturbing past as part of their life story and therefore it was challenging to discover the key leadership development area that guided each woman into the arena of leadership.

Young Kim did not rise up as a leader in her own right until she was widowed. Prior to this, a key development related to the honing of her skills. Young Kim is, by her own admission, generally an even-tempered person but in the overall plan it seems that her acquisition and practice of her skills were the keys to her leadership. Kim Cho led a good, comfortable life but was an inward-looking person until Jesus captured her heart. Her character development related to being compassionate was key to Kim Cho's leadership as it compelled her to look beyond herself.

For Indians Priscilla and Ruth, and Singaporean Pushpamani, having mentors who guided them into leadership was a key leadership development area. In addition, the possibilities shown to Priscilla through this mentoring gave her confidence and hope that it would be possible for her to serve in many ways in the kingdom of God.

Singaporean Lydia's willingness to venture into new service was key to her leadership development. She did this when she became a founding member of a new church plant in her country. The other two Singaporeans, Kat and Alice, and Malaysian Elizabeth had a similar but contextually different development area. Their inner understanding of God's gift to them of leadership was a significant development area in their lives. For Kat, understanding this gift of leadership came in a ministry context while for Alice, it was in the context of her current motherhood season. Elizabeth's inner understanding that leadership was her gift allowed her to assume leadership positions from her childhood days.

RA's inner transformation and the understanding of her call contributed to her development as a pioneer leader for Arab women.

Character development is also a major part of the entire leadership development process and this aspect will be explored in the next chapter. Another major development area is related to education and this is presented in the separate section below.

Opportunities for Service as Leaders in Christian Ministry

Table 8 above also lists the leadership opportunities available for these women as professionals and in Christian communities. Among the four missionaries who shared their narratives, one was a former ordained pastor who is now a mother. From childhood to adolescence to adulthood, opportunities were available if the women were willing to assume the responsibilities. In Elizabeth's case, the family and community expected her to lead by caring for her younger siblings when she was a child. Priscilla, who did not even realize that Sunday school teachers are considered as leaders in the community, looked upon teachers as helpers until she was corrected by her female mentor.

The most significant time of leadership seems to be adulthood, but this is dependent on other factors such as individual call, character and spiritual formation submitted to the conformity of Christ's image. The women's willingness to invest their time, efforts and lives to advance God's kingdom was directly connected to their growth and opportunities received for the exercise of their leadership gift.

The narratives indicate that the women were able to operate at local, national and regional levels for ministry. For example, Lydia, who was a founding member of a church plant in Singapore, also served in short-term missions in other Asian nations. Priscilla and Ruth are ministers both in their host and their home nations. They use a portion of their annual holidays to disciple believers when they return to visit their parents in India.

All of the women except Elizabeth are married and are also mothers. Out of the nine mothers, three are grandmothers. The only mother with very young children is Alice. A marked difference exists between the freedom available to mothers with grown-up children and mothers with very young children. As a former pastor who had leadership responsibilities and authority, Alice answered her call to be a missionary with confidence because she understood her call. However, when she married and became a mother, she needed to understand that "being a mother is also being a leader."

Yet it is interesting to note that, except for Elizabeth who is a salaried pastor, the rest are volunteers and do not receive a wage for their service. The volunteers raised their own financial support and have served in various unpaid capacities and ministered as mothers within their families. Some of the roles and responsibilities of these women warrant better recognition by the Asian Church and Asian Christian male leaders.

Educational Opportunities and Lifelong Learning Attitudes

All of the ten Asian Christian women servant-leaders have had the opportunity at various times in their lives to attend school or university, or be theologically trained.

Young Kim graduated with a pharmacy degree and her only form of further training in the Bible came many years later when she attended the theological courses that her husband was taking while they were preparing to become missionaries. She remembered, "Before we [Young Kim and her husband, now deceased] were sent out as missionaries, we did a six-month internship in a seminary in New York. I was attending courses with Sam." Young Kim thinks that she does not need seminary training at her age since her spiritual gifts are already being used for the global church.

Elizabeth decided to enroll herself in Methodist Theological School when she was twenty-three-plus years old because she wanted to become a pastor. She continued with her Bachelor of Art in Theology in 2002 and graduated in 2005 with the degree.

Table 9 provides a summary of the educational environments that were crucial to their growth as Christian servant-leaders. Some attended formal theological training while others either attended informal or had non-formal theological training.

Table 9: Educational Development of Asian Christian Women Servant-Leaders

Educational Paths	Number of Women
From Christian schools (elementary/high school/ university) to theological training (formal and non-formal)	4
From non-Christian schools (elementary/high school/ university) to theological training (formal and non-formal)	3
From Christian schools (elementary/high school/ university) to informal Bible training	3

As the ten women grew in faith and hungered to know God better, at least seven of them engaged in formal or non-formal theological education, acquiring a diploma or degree.

Kim Cho, who was not a believer in the beginning but excelled in Christian education in her Christian school, went on to study theology in her forties. She would subsequently acquire a doctoral degree in missions in her fifties. Elizabeth and Alice, who came from non-Christian backgrounds, received Jesus and went on to theological education to serve as pastor at an East Malaysian church and missionary to a restricted nation, respectively.

In journeying to obey God's call in their lives, these Asian Christian women servant-leaders experienced various events that shaped their understanding as leaders. Educational opportunities were life opportunities that positioned these women to rise up to serve as leaders.

Discussion

Keys to understanding the journey to leadership from the Asian Christian women leaders' perspectives and the emphasis on education as a major entrance point into various opportunities are part of this discussion.

The Asian Christian Woman's Journey to Leadership

Ten Asian Christian women servant-leaders shared about their obedience to answer the call to rise up as leaders. Young Kim had the leadership gifting but did not rise up till she stepped into her pastor-husband's shoes without the official recognition due to a pastor. Kim Cho found her leadership gifting at a later age and pursued theological education that would be an open door to quick acceptance among other male leaders. Priscilla began to soar in ministry when she grasped a deep understanding of the Great Commission. Ruth's faith increased when she understood the deeper meaning of God's righteousness through biblical education and mentoring, and now she helps others to do the same. Octogenarian Pushpamani led Bible study groups and seized every opportunity to talk about Jesus to others during her days on earth. Lydia pursued biblical education after age sixty and is serving actively as a Bible study leader for a women's group. Kat was a church-planting team member and continues to be in the church leadership. Alice ministers as a mother to her children and is bringing them up in godly ways. Elizabeth became a seminary lecturer after many years as a pastor of local churches, and RA began her own regional ministry to Arab women. All of these women have testimonies full of God's love, grace and commission to disciple among the nations.

The narratives of the ten Asian Christian women servant-leaders give hope to many other women who may not understand their call, their leadership development which God begins from childhood, and the constant and consistent opportunities to serve in the kingdom of God. Willingness to submit to and obey God is just one of the keys which unlocks the door to limitless opportunities. Asian Christian women servant-leaders need not be limited in their dreams to serve God. They are able to share their gifts, under the leadership of the Holy Spirit, in "Jerusalem, Judea and Samaria" (Acts 1:8).

Asian Christian women servant-leaders who have a pastoral calling have demonstrated that they are not limited in using their gifts. They find creative ways to exercise their gifts. However, in a general Asian context, men who are called to be pastors are usually identified and encouraged to pursue equipping in a theological institution. In addition, they are appointed and ordained as pastors. They would also be paid a decent wage for their vocation. The Asian Church will greatly benefit if women who are called to be pastors are similarly encouraged and provided with theological training. In addition, the Asian Church should exercise fairness in appointing and ordaining women as pastors, thus giving full recognition, authority and remuneration to these women who minister for the Lord Jesus.

Among the other keys are renewal of the earthly mind to a kingdom mindset, a self-understanding that one possesses the gift of leadership, a willingness to be mentored into leadership, increased faith, and theological or biblical education. A larger sample of narratives might yield other factors that contribute to Asian Christian women's leadership growth.

Education for Asian Christian Women

The leadership development process of the ten Asian Christian women servant-leaders does not seem to be drastically different from the leadership development process that Clinton or Glanville discussed from Western perspectives.[9] However, I would emphasize that the Asian Christian women leaders in these interviews have shown a keen interest in being theologically sound. It seems that education, both secular and theological, has opened doors for them. This is significant as many Asian women do not have the opportunity to be educated; thus, the challenge of raising women servant-leaders from poorer communities or those where education is less accessible can be overcome by offering theological studies.

One area of education for Christian women would be a comprehensive understanding of motherhood as a ministry period. Women might benefit from being taught that mothers are also servant-leaders. Whether women servant-leaders focus on being a mother or continue to extend their gifts to the Christian community during their motherhood phase would be a choice made in obedience to God's voice.

Summary

This chapter discussed the types of calling of each woman with reference to Ephesians 4:11–12. These women's narratives were further analyzed for categories of development and this yielded four main categories: character development, mental development, physical development and spiritual development were all part of the leadership development. These Asian Christian women servant-leaders had opportunities to study theology in formal, non-formal and informal settings that yielded better-equipped servants of Christ.

The women's obedience to their call and their willingness to journey in servant-leadership for Christ's sake gives hope to the Asian Church which may yet become one of the most promising and powerful Christ-centered bodies for such a time as this.

---

9. Clinton, *The Making*; Glanville, "Leadership Development."

9

Christian Leadership According to the Narratives

Perceptions are influenced by a variety of factors. How do Asian Christian women servant-leaders define Christian leadership? What are some of the leadership challenges they face and how do they overcome them? It is important to note that perceptions of Christian leadership will be seen through the theological and cultural lenses worn by the ten women as they narrate their life stories. Although these women were from different Asian nations, some wore similar theological and cultural lenses, while others from the same nation thought and voiced their perspectives on Christian leadership differently.

The eight qualities of humility, love, intimacy with God, faith in God, acceptance of diversity, stewardship, trustworthiness and pursuit of unity mentioned in chapter 4 will be used as markers as we listen to the voices of these women.

Definition of Christian Leadership According to Asian Christian Women Servant-Leaders

According to the narratives, all the women assumed that individual or corporate Christian leadership would primarily be centered on Jesus Christ as their Lord and Savior. All of the women had an instinct that it is allowable for women to become and serve as leaders and had a view of what it means to be a Christian leader.

A majority of the women believed that Christian leadership is sacrificial service and leaders have a goal to mobilize others for Christ. For example, Alice remarked, "Christian leadership would mean that a leader will be someone who influences another Christian or non-Christian towards Christ." Alice

115

considered herself a leader as she was influencing her children for Christ. She reminisced that when she was a pastor, she had preached from the pulpit, thereby influencing hundreds of worshippers.

I found RA and Elizabeth to be the most forceful about their views on Christian leadership. RA said these words with passion and pain:

> In our part of this world, true Christian leadership does not exist because it's a "man thing," you know, especially in the church. Christian leadership means a pastor is expected to be right always and live in a godly way all the time. But you know, in this part [of the world] . . . the role of the women is really remotely related to Christian leadership. Even the wife of the minister [pastor] is expected to be perfect and do everything without saying a word and without being involved in decisions, or consultations. She is hardly given the chance to be trained or the opportunities [to minister] with the same regard as the male minister. Leadership revolves around the men.

Elizabeth echoed, "God made us equal . . . God made Adam first and Eve second, but that does not mean Adam is higher [in position] than Eve. Eve is a partner with Adam. We must think positive[ly], we are partners with the men."

While Kim Cho emphasized that Christian leadership is about service and sacrifice, Kat added a reminder that the leader influences others to "do everything for Christ." According to Kat, the Christian leader "is somebody who follows Jesus and causes other people to follow him through their life witness."

Table 10 sets out the perspectives of the ten Asian Christian women servant-leaders regarding Christian leadership.

Eight women cited that Christian leadership demands an attitude of selfless service from leaders who are focused on directing people to our Lord Jesus Christ and his teachings. In the process of Christian leadership, the leaders are expected to engage other Christians to remain active in ministry for Jesus Christ. Kat is an example of a Christian leader who engages in evangelism and discipleship in her home nation as well as in other nations. She was a founding member of a church plant in her home nation and also helped to begin an orphanage in India. In addition, she has been instrumental in her work environment by beginning a fellowship for medical staff in a major hospital in her home nation. Pushpamani remarked, "Leadership is servanthood," acknowledging that serving others must be of top interest and priority for Christian leaders.

Table 10: Perspectives on Christian Leadership as Understood by the Asian Christian Women Servant-Leaders

Perspectives on Christian Leadership	Number of Citations
Christian leadership is sacrificial service, mobilization of people for Christ and leading/influencing people to Christ	8
Christian leadership is about accepting challenges and being responsible for the consequences	2
Christian leadership is teamwork and togetherness	1
Christian leadership is about having a lifelong learning attitude	1
Christian leadership is about being a mother at home and engaging in discipleship of the children	1
Christian leadership is equal for both men and women	1
True Christian leadership does not exist (in the sense of only men being considered as leaders and not women)	1

Two women viewed that accepting challenges and being responsible for personal actions are aspects of leadership. Leadership was also about working together as a team, having a lifelong learning attitude and being a mother and discipling children.

RA, the Jordanian, had a strong view that "true Christian leadership does not exist," reflecting a personal frustration whereby women in her church were not allowed to excel as servant-leaders. This frustration was deepened as she reflected on her status as a pastor's wife. Her remark also implies that she believes in equality in leadership roles. In line with RA's statement and in reference to the other narratives, a total of nine out of ten interviewees have experienced this personal frustration whereby only men are allowed to be leaders and women are barred from any leadership positions and experiences.

Leadership Qualities of Asian Christian Women Leaders

The eight leadership qualities of humility, love, intimacy with God, faith in God, acceptance of diversity, stewardship, trustworthiness and pursuit of unity were used as markers for analyzing the ten Asian Christian women's narratives. While these women are strong leaders, there is always the possibility that their narratives may not highlight some of these qualities. These selected eight characteristics of biblical leadership were chosen and used to analyze the leadership qualities of the women because they aptly showcase the characteristics found in Christian leaders; these qualities were modeled in a twentieth-century Asian Christian woman leader, Pandita Ramabai, throughout her life dedicated to Christ.

Elizabeth is an example of someone who understood her imperfection and the depth of God's love for her when she accepted Christ as Lord and Savior. She followed God's call as a pastor and has remained faithful. During her days as a new believer, other Christians had encouraged her. Thus, she has done the same for others through the years of her ministry. She said, "I try to encourage them [believers and especially other leaders regardless of gender] in how God uses us and leads us." Elizabeth is an encourager. Her accomplishment as a pastor who plans and mobilizes people to achieve goals makes her a visionary, an influencer and a mobilizer for Christ.

Table 11 reveals that the Asian Christian women servant-leaders possessed these eight qualities, which surfaced during the verbal interactions. Christian leaders with these qualities will also be service-oriented. For Ruth, the combination of humility, intimacy with God and faith in God allowed her to enjoy guidance from God. The qualities of love and stewardship would propel the leader into service. Here the servant-leader is expected to use her spiritual gifts with the love of God. The consequence of being a trustworthy or dependable leader is that it establishes the spiritual authority of the leader and encourages the leader to serve better. Only one interviewee, Young Kim, was concerned that the exercise of leadership by women should not cause any dissension. Her pursuit of unity would result in peace.

In addition, two more qualities emerged, namely vision and boldness. Being visionary and being bold are qualities that four women expected of themselves. These qualities allowed them to serve others, possess authority and provided self-confidence. Two Indian leaders (Ruth and Priscilla) based in the Middle East had clear ministry visions. Two Singaporean leaders shared information that highlighted their own bold personalities.

Table 11: Christian Leadership Qualities Possessed by Asian Christian Women Leaders

Qualities	Citations through Narratives	Consequences
Humility	• I asked God and he showed me the correct direction for my life (Ruth). • I made myself available according to the season of my time . . . And whatever came to hand, I did on condition that it was within my abilities to do and I was comfortable enough to do so (Kat). • My forte was music, so they [Christian friends] asked me to play for their home group. I played for them (Lydia).	Guidance Service Service
Love	• [I wanted to] tackle the issues that women needed to know about as Christian women and [as non-Christian] women who are talented and equipped but they [their gifts, talents and time] are not used. At the same time, not in a revolutionary way, but in love and understanding, [I wanted to] make their voice heard (RA). • I have a heart for the people and I always pray for them (Kim Cho).	Service Service
Intimacy with God	• I asked God and he showed me the correct direction for my life (Ruth). • I made myself available according to the season of my time . . . And whatever came to hand, I did on condition that it was within my abilities to do and I was comfortable enough to do so (Kat). • I started to become close to God, like avoiding sin in my life (Priscilla). • I had the desire that, one day, I wanted to serve the Lord. And I worked towards it through the help of God (Pushpamani). • I have a heart for the people and I always pray for them (Kim Cho). • I always pray to God and God always gives me the strength and wisdom to overcome (Elizabeth).	Guidance Service Purity Service Service Strength and wisdom

Qualities	Citations through Narratives	Consequences
Faith in God	• I asked God and he showed me the correct direction for my life (Ruth).	Guidance
	• I made myself available according to the season of my time . . . And whatever came to hand, I did on condition that it was within my abilities to do and I was comfortable enough to do so (Kat).	Service
	• I had the desire that, one day, I wanted to serve the Lord. And I worked towards it through the help of God (Pushpamani).	Service
	• I am an optimistic person; God made me this way (Kim Cho).	Self-confidence
	• I always pray to God and God always gives me the strength and wisdom to overcome (Elizabeth).	Strength and wisdom
Acceptance of diversity	• Part of that is to equip others so that they will be suited for God's purposes in this country (Ruth).	Service
	• You need to be really kind even to the lowest, the sweeper [at the hospital] (Lydia).	Service
	• I am a missionary and have a heart for Muslim women (Kim Cho).	Service
	• I am an optimistic person; God made me this way. The moment I realized that I was saved, I had more reason to live in this world. Not just for myself, but for others (Kim Cho).	Service
Stewardship	• I wanted to be a role model and to walk and experience this journey in leadership in the right way (RA).	Service
	• Part of that is to equip others so that they will be suited for God's purposes in this country (Ruth).	Service
	• Through [this teaching and discipling], I am able to bring up many women leaders (Priscilla).	Service
	• I made myself available according to the season of my time . . . And whatever came to hand, I did on condition that it was within my abilities to do and I was comfortable enough to do so (Kat).	Service

Qualities	Citations through Narratives	Consequences
Stewardship (con't)	• [I believe that] we [can] influence our circle where we are and they [others] will recognize me as a leader (Young Kim).	Service
	• The moment I realized that I was saved, I had more reason to live in this world. Not just for myself but for others (Kim Cho).	Service
	• At a 1996 Methodist Women Annual Conference, I shared my experience and encouraged the women. [I told them] that God leads and uses us (Elizabeth).	Service
Trust-worthiness	• There was one incident where I was leading the youth and she interrupted [me] and took over. [She did this] because she thought that I was not able to perform a particular task. Later I had a chat with her, I was young then [about sixteen years old]. I thought that I needed to tell her how I felt [about her interrupting my leadership]. She apologized [to me] and this was good. She accepted what I said and she did not do it again (Alice).	Spiritual authority
	• Half of the Sunday school responsibilities came to me (Priscilla).	Spiritual authority
	• My forte was music, so they [Christian friends] asked me to play for their home group. I played for them (Lydia).	Service
	• It is boldness and integrity. I was in charge of my ward of forty-five patients. I needed to be honest, truthful and show kindness (Lydia).	Authority* and service
Pursuit of unity	• Because we are ladies, we need to think wisely [about how we exercise our leadership] . . . Too much aggression as a [female leader] will likely make situations worse (Young Kim).	Peace

* Lydia was not a Christian when she held the position of a nurse, thus she did not have spiritual authority

According to the Asian Christian women servant-leaders, Christian leaders are to be self-sacrificial and Christ-focused in their service, and are expected to mobilize people to Christ by leading and influencing them. Asian Christian women viewed servant-leadership as being accessible to both men and women, that mothers are servant-leaders, and that Christian women leaders ought to have a lifelong attitude towards learning and endeavor to work as a team. These Asian Christian women have been affirmed in leadership but, like any male leader, they have also experienced challenges.

Challenges to Asian Christian Women's Leadership Growth

The discussion of leadership challenges encountered as Christian servant-leaders was intense and painful for the women. Some were visibly frustrated as they revisited these challenges. Yet it was also a time of healing as some of these women, inevitably, realized that God had taken them through these personal challenges and established them in their respective ministries. I would at times stop to enquire if the women had forgiven those who had hurt them. It was an outflow of the fellowship we enjoyed as the women shared their experiences. These women did not feel offended by such a query.

The ten Asian Christian women servant-leaders encountered challenges from various contexts – cultural, spiritual, theological, family, gender, relational and others. A combination of these major categories became challenges to their growth as servant-leaders. Some of these women also experienced other minor challenges that have been categorized as "other challenges."

Elizabeth, the ordained pastor, felt discouraged when especially her fellow colleagues, who were mostly male pastors, did not appreciate her successful endeavors. She commented that her culture was weak because men do not support a woman as a leader.

RA, who established a regional ministry reaching out to Arab women, was also discouraged when church leaders (including pastors) did not or were unable to recognize a woman's giftings and talents. She said that, culturally, "there are some men who are not willing to shake hands with the women." Some men (pastors and church leaders) would not allow a woman wearing accessories to partake in Holy Communion. Still, RA understood and respected the fact that her denomination would not allow women to lead in worship or preach from the pulpit as the teachings are "mixed with culture and religious teaching. We live under the influence of Islamic culture . . . in their [pastors' and church leaders'] background, they have Islamic culture living in them.

They are no different from the Muslim family." RA revealed that the influence of Islamic culture is brought into the church and can be seen in the way that pastors and church leaders treat women.

Kim Cho remarked that the older South Korean generation does not allow women to serve as leaders and they are people influenced by Confucianism. Therefore, Korean Christians' perspectives about women may be directly related to the bigger socio-cultural worldview of women. Kim Cho mentions that Confucianism is still prevailing.[1]

Priscilla felt that gender was the main issue. She too was discouraged but by immature believers who, in their cultural context, could not accept her spiritual leadership. She was granted leadership responsibilities but found herself "running" to her husband for decisions as that would validate her husband's "headship" over her.

Table 12 lists the challenges faced by Asian Christian women servant-leaders as they pursue service in a Christian environment.

Table 12: Challenges Faced by Asian Christian Women Leaders to Their Growth and Ministry as Servant-Leaders

Types of Challenges	Number of Citations
Cultural – relates to the social behavior of a community	7
Spiritual – relates to the inner person: emotions, character and spiritual authority	7
Family – relates to parents and children living in a household	5
Theological – relates to the scriptural interpretation of women in leadership	3
Gender – relates to the state of being male or female	3
Relational – relates to relationships between individuals or generations	3
Other challenges: Lack of encouragement from male ministry colleagues Cognitive challenge related to struggling with the acceptance and understanding of the concept "A mother is a leader." Slow pace of change	2 1 1

---

1. South Korea elected its first female president in 2013 despite the prevailing influence of Confucianism.

Cultural challenges relate to the community's ideas, customs and behavior towards their women. Spiritual challenges relate to how a Christian is affected in his or her inner being, emotions and character while being aligned with God. Persecution could be categorized as a spiritual challenge as it affects the emotions and faith of the one persecuted. The persecuted person is treated with hostility because of her belief in Christ. Family challenges relate to the negative attitudes and lack of support shown by parents, spouses or children towards these women in servant-leadership. Theological challenges refer mainly to either the complementarian or egalitarian thoughts discussed earlier in this book. Gender challenges relate to how women see themselves as ministry leaders in a male or patriarchal environment. Relational challenges refer to any kind of relational difficulties between individuals or generations (older generation versus younger generation) and within organizations. The last category was simply termed "other challenges": these citations were few and did not fit the other broader categories.

In describing her spiritual challenge, RA confessed that she rushes too much, and therefore forgets to pause for Christ. This affects her ability to make decisions that will please God and sometimes she is pressured to please people. Priscilla discussed the challenge to spiritual authority and stated that this happened due to the "immaturity of church members. There was unnecessary backbiting and criticism." Kat's spiritual challenges related to the lack of dependency on God and challenges to spiritual authority. The latter challenge stands in contrast to Kat's education, profession and leadership in an egalitarian church.

Ruth's challenges, experienced during her adolescence, could be categorized as persecutions. In the first persecution, her parents beat her for questioning their worship of saints. In the second persecution, Ruth had fellowshipped with an Indian Muslim convert to Christianity. Other Muslim students and teachers assumed that it was because of Ruth that this young lady had converted. Ruth and a few other Christian students were threatened with expulsion. Ruth especially was locked in her dormitory room with no food or drink. Her faith was challenged.

The "busy mother syndrome" is a challenge to ministry leadership and especially to young mothers like Alice. This refers to the lack of time or division of time for family and ministry.

RA had the loudest voice with regards to theological challenges. Cultural, theological and gender challenges were infused in RA's world. RA's own church does not allow women to lead worship or preach at services. She viewed leadership differently and exclaimed that Christian leadership for women does not exist as leadership is reserved only for the men. The women, apparently, are "far away from Christian leadership."

An example of a relational challenge given by Kim Cho concerns the generational differences between the older and younger generations in Korean culture. The older Koreans are not able to accept a female pastor in the church, while the younger generation are more accepting and welcoming of female pastors.

The tone and thread of discouragement and disappointment weighs heavily in the voices of these Asian Christian women servant-leaders. Discouragement stems from the lack of support from some spouses, lack of recognition of women leaders by most male pastors and church leaders, criticism of their leadership from other women, other women's lack of courage to speak out or come forward as leaders, the culture's neglect of women or denial of gender equality, and, in some cases according to the narratives, the theological interpretation of women in leadership.

Management of Challenges Experienced by Asian Christian Women Servant-Leaders

The uniqueness of the ten Asian Christian women servant-leaders in terms of their cultural, theological and spiritual contexts provided passive and active ways to manage or overcome their challenges. Priscilla's narrative reveals some of these ways of managing or overcoming challenges.

Priscilla faced challenges in ministry when male leaders questioned her decision-making process. Another challenge was that some female co-workers would not rise to give their best in ministry. Her husband has been her greatest cheerleader. Priscilla narrated an incident when male leaders would bypass her authority as the Sunday school headmistress and consult her husband (who was a Sunday school teacher) for a decision pertaining to this ministry. Her husband helped her by referring the male leaders back to Priscilla. On a personal front, her own renewal in mind came about as she understood that Sunday school teachers are leaders. In the cultural and religious environment of women like Priscilla, Sunday school teachers are not acknowledged as leaders. Priscilla admitted, "Our Sunday school teachers were not considered as potential leaders. I still remember when sister Rachel asked me, 'What ministry do you do?' I said, 'Nothing,' but she found out that I did Sunday school teaching. I did not realize that it was a ministry or that I am a leader [until she pointed it out to me]."[2]

Priscilla continued to upgrade her education by completing a diploma in Practical Ministry with Biblical Education by Extension Korea. Her thankfulness is seen as she declared, "Education – biblical education – developed me and gave me confidence . . . the Word of God gave me confidence."

The next step for Priscilla was to obey God's Word and to make disciples of all nations. Her spiritual fruit is evident as she has "trained around sixty to seventy people in the last four years. Most are leaders and 50 percent [of the students] are men. They are Indian expatriates working in the Middle East. They come from different churches. Serving as a facilitator really enhanced my leadership. After becoming a facilitator, I started standing [became established] as a leader."

In this regard, it seems that practically all the women overcame their challenges with similar approaches of prayer, dependence on God's Word and simply leaning into the embrace of Christ. Elizabeth overcomes her challenges by praying for God's strength and wisdom, accepting the moral support from her family and friends, and sometimes taking time out to retreat and rest before God.

In Table 13, a passive response refers to a process within their minds and hearts. Passive responses (six citations) related to cultural and theological challenges outnumbered passive responses to other challenges. This suggests that Asian women servant-leaders are most affected by their cultural and theological environment's influence on the perception of women in Christian leadership. They were internally trying to process their own struggles related to how they were being viewed as servant-leaders in their own cultural and theological environments.

The women acknowledged the need to understand and accept their culture, with one woman being most passive when she said, "Just follow and be the helper" (Young Kim), which in our interaction context meant, "Accept the situation, do not fight it." At least two women felt strongly that Asian Christian women need to have proper theological training so that they can minister to men and be accepted as teachers, especially by older men. A couple of women

---

2. I had the pleasure of discipling Priscilla and her husband for six years from 2005 to 2011. In addition, in Priscilla's church culture, only the pastor and his executive team were acknowledged as leaders because they made executive decisions. Men and women who were Sunday school teachers were not seen as decision-makers and therefore not worthy to be acknowledged as leaders. Priscilla realized that she was making decisions, influencing and leading young children and the youth, and that made her a leader.

suggested that co-educational Bible studies and ministry co-operation would be beneficial for both men and women.

Table 13: Overcoming Leadership Challenges Faced by Asian Christian Women Servant-Leaders

Types of Challenges	Ways to Overcome Challenges (Number of Citations) Passive Responses	Ways to Overcome Challenges (Number of Citations) Active Responses
Cultural	(a) Understanding and respecting existing cultural and theological stance (1) (b) Recognizing that love and grace must be above the law (1) (c) Just following and being the helper – accepting the situation (1)	(a) Having a proper theological education (2) (b) Showing believers how God thinks of women (1) (c) Men and women studying or training together (2) (d) Pastor acknowledging the woman leader in ministry (1)
Spiritual	(a) Recognizing that love and grace must be above the law (1) (b) Reflecting on fruits of the ministry (1)	(a) Focusing on God's call and direction (2) (b) Depending on God (5) (c) Experiencing joy upon reflecting on fruits of ministry (1)
Family	(a) Recognizing that the season of motherhood will pass (1)	(a) Receiving positive encouragement to pursue leadership from spouse, family and other encouragers (10) (b) Receiving exhortation from husband during motherhood season (1) (c) Managing time between family and ministry during motherhood season (3)

Types of Challenges	Ways to Overcome Challenges (Number of Citations) Passive Responses	Ways to Overcome Challenges (Number of Citations) Active Responses
Theological	(a) Understanding and respecting existing cultural and theological stance (1) (b) Thinking positively that men and women are partners in ministry. God made Adam and Eve equal (1) (c) Recognizing that love and grace must be above the law (1)	(a) Having a proper theological education (1) (b) Showing believers how God thinks of women (1) (c) Pastor acknowledging the woman leader in ministry (1)
Gender	(a) Knowing that women can be effective and influential (1)	(a) Women having self-confidence and speaking out (1) (b) Pastor acknowledging the woman leader in ministry (1)
Relational		(a) Revisiting the basics – being humble and loving (1) (b) Trusting God for grace and love for people (1)
Other challenges		(a) Believing in self to make the change, and making the change (1) (b) Engaging in lifelong learning (2) (c) Persevering to complete tasks (1)

The most important key to overcoming spiritual challenges is to wholly depend on God. Prayer and finding comfort in/from the Scriptures were the most used spiritual disciplines during difficult times and challenges. A focus on God's call and keeping in step with God's direction were ways that helped them in overcoming challenges.

The support base of these strong Asian Christian women servant-leaders consisted of all or one of these groups of people: family, friends and encouragers (mentors, motivators and role models). This has been an important factor in all of their lives as they have handled family challenges. Balancing family and ministry life is tricky but not impossible, as some women feel that good time management will allow them to serve better.

The women value moral support from family members, friends and the church community. In particular, married women leaders were relieved that their husbands supported their service as leaders in ministries. The women's honor is strongly tied to their acknowledgment as leaders in ministries. This acknowledgment, according to the women's narratives, is expressed through prayers pertaining to them and their ministries, and appreciative words given in recognition of their efforts.

Asian Christian women leaders also view education, whether biblical or secular, to be important in their growth as leaders of ministries. In fact, all the women have accomplished some sort of biblical or theological training.

It was interesting that only two women expressed that change had to happen in oneself before it can impact or influence others. Yet the narratives indicate that all of the women are strong leaders and role models of Christian faith and therefore imply that change had to happen within themselves too. This belief has helped the Asian Christian women servant-leaders to position their self-esteem and identity firmly in Christ.

As disciple-makers who invest their lives in the lives of others, these Asian Christian women servant-leaders were aware of the need to role model their absolute faith in a God who would deliver them from these challenges. They role modeled their obedience and trust in God by responding in godly ways. For example, Elizabeth, who was clearly disappointed that a majority of the male pastors did not offer any encouragement towards the ministry given to her, did not carry any bitterness towards their (the male pastors') actions. Instead she quickly remembered two foreign male pastors who had encouraged her to persevere in ministry.

All of the women servant-leaders went through challenges that shaped them to become better leaders. The women's leadership was mostly culturally and theologically challenged. Some women worked within the contexts of these challenges but with disappointment, while others broke through the barriers and helped other Christian men and women to understand the possibilities for Christian women servant-leadership in Asia.

Discussion

In this discussion, I bring out key concerns related to leadership perspectives as revealed through the narratives of the ten Asian Christian women servant-leaders. These women servant-leaders are in different nations in Asia and yet they seem to face similar challenges to their leadership. The theological and cultural contexts as well as the issue of gender are challenges that need to be overcome with wisdom, love and unity.

Asian Christian Women as Servant-Leaders

In the definition of Christian leadership from the perspective of Western male leaders, some key words and phrases emerged: influencing others towards accomplishment, accountability, God-given ability and responsibilities, and readiness to pursue a vision. The Asian Christian women leaders agree with this definition of leadership defined from a Western male perspective because it is also biblically sound. In fact, one Asian voice (Alice) thinks that being a mother is also being a leader, which is in agreement with Professor Elizabeth Glanville's conclusion in her unpublished dissertation.

There was one more item to be added to the Asian Christian women servant-leaders' perspective of leadership. This journey must account for equality in leadership for men and women. With regard to the thought about equality, the women's voices became louder when discussing challenges to their leadership. Asian Christian women servant-leaders strongly believe that Christian leadership roles, skills and qualities of servant-leaders are meant to be for both men and women who follow Jesus Christ.

Their expectation is that all who are appropriately qualified should be given the opportunities to serve Jesus without any discrimination or prejudice. This view aligns itself more with the egalitarian perspective of women in leadership than with the Asian feminist theological approach. According to the narratives, the women have been working and continue to work in unity with men to bring about transformation and advancement in the kingdom of God. Except for RA, who began a women's organization because both her denomination and cultural background limited her, all the other nine women understood patriarchy but were focused on their gifts and calling as servant-leaders. They received empowerment and moral encouragement from both men and women, and acquired a biblical understanding of their roles as kingdom servant-leaders.

The Asian Christian women leaders' definition of biblical leadership may be stated in the following way:

> Biblical leadership is a lifelong learning process of becoming self-sacrificial, responsible and influential so that more people can be mobilized and impacted for our Lord Jesus Christ, and it is accessible for both men and women.

The ten Asian Christian women leaders are strong and godly leaders, and therefore it is not a surprise to see the revelation or expression of the eight leadership qualities in their narratives. Two more interrelated qualities – being visionary and being bold – emerged. These are important qualities for the Asian

Christian women who come from a theological, cultural or religious context that suppresses the voice of emerging female Christian servant-leaders. Having a vision for ministry indicates that God speaks to women and gifts them with leadership and authority to carry out the vision. Visionary Asian Christian women servant-leaders need the boldness born out of intimacy and faith in God to pursue their call.

Breakthroughs, Contextual Submission and Louder Voices

The narratives of these ten Asian Christian women servant-leaders have shown that to be a servant-leader, one needs to persevere against all odds. Generally, when the cultural or theological contexts dictate that Asian women should not hold leadership positions or carry out leadership responsibilities above men, they may respond in one of two ways: (1) the women understand the stance and do not rise up in leadership; or (2) they understand the stance and are creative in their leadership. They may also respond in one of two ways when a culture and theology permit women to be leaders according to God's will: (1) the women choose not to grow as leaders; or (2) the women engage by equipping themselves so that they can be great leaders.

The ten Asian Christian women servant-leaders were challenged by cultural and denominational practices, together with gender discrimination. Initially, the women experienced a sense of voicelessness and low self-esteem until they resisted with the truth found in the Scriptures. They then found solace through prayer and encouragement from their support group comprised of individuals who knew and cared about them. In addition, these women strongly believed that changes in attitudes, and how one thinks of self, begins with oneself. They were determined to change the course of condemnation to one of inspiration, demonstrating their interest in being recognized for their gifts and talents. They desired to find ways to work together with men more than engage in or debate on theological issues that hindered their growth as leaders.

Through the narratives, we see that the Asian Christian women servant-leaders demonstrated the following:

- Obedience to Christ through their call is primary;
- Leaders who break through cultural or theological norms that inhibit women will face discouragement and disappointments, but those norms can be overcome with patience and perseverance;
- God will give creative ways to manage or overcome these challenges;

- Asian Christian women leaders have the potential to reflect God's power and when led by God's Spirit have great opportunities to impact the nations of this world.

Summary

The ten Asian Christian women servant-leaders' understanding of Christian leadership and of leadership qualities, which each woman possessed, were drawn from the narratives. Their residence in different parts of Asia was challenged mostly culturally and theologically in reference to their leadership in Christian communities. However, their perseverance to manage or overcome these challenges affirms their call to serve through their leadership gifting by God.

10

Opinions

In this book, I endeavor to express the unique position of Asian Christian women servant-leaders in voicing their ministry leadership growth, opportunities and challenges. The voice of Asian Christian women servant-leaders needs to be recognized, accepted and made stronger by Asian Christian churches, and I hope that this book will create some awareness so that a majority Christian force can be effectively harnessed for kingdom work nationally, regionally and globally.

The last four chapters presented the narratives of ten Asian Christian women servant-leaders and contributed to some recommendations that would be useful for emerging Asian Christian women servant-leaders, Asian Christian male servant-leaders and cross-cultural missionaries who serve in Asian nations among Asian groups.

This chapter will include some advice from the ten women, my personal ministry commitment to give a louder voice to Asian Christian women leaders, and other recommendations that it might be useful for the larger Asian Church community to consider, correct and contribute for the completion of the Great Commission through Asian Christian women leaders.

The Responses

The responses are related to discovering the Asian context that shaped the opportunities and challenges for the ten selected Asian Christian women servant-leaders; the biblical principles of leadership that are embodied by them; the definition of Christian leadership from an Asian Christian female perspective; the development patterns for Asian evangelical Christian women in leadership; and the key opportunities or challenges in leadership growth.

The Influence of Culture and Theology

Asian cultural perspectives include parental influence and the value of education in children's lives. The role that parents adopt in their families is important; in particular, godly parents have a responsibility to raise godly children. Secular and theological education opens doors to recognition and service. These influences allow women to progress in life as well as to fulfil the call to disciple the nations.

Discipling Begins in the Family

> Train up a child in the way he should go;
> even when he is old he will not depart from it. (Prov 22:6)

Asian parents exert both authority and influence on their children. This cultural context is advantageous for kingdom expansion when well-discipled Christian parents are able to exert a godly influence on their children. In Asia, the generation of twenty- to forty-year-olds is the generation that is likely to see marriages, build families and in some cases experience divorce. This is also the next generation of leadership in the churches, which requires intentional Christian discipleship. In this twenty-first century, the next generation's emerging servant-leaders would benefit greatly if the church practiced the multiplication principle: "What you have heard from me in the presence of many witnesses entrust to faithful men who will be able to teach others also" (2 Tim 2:2).

This is not to say that the Asian Church is not practicing the multiplication principle, but simply to encourage the church to revisit the Great Commission and the 2 Timothy 2:2 principle with focus and determination. My own understanding of this need as well as God's call on my life has caused me to align my ministry focus on the next generation of Christian leaders – both young men and young women. In addition, Asian Church pastors and leaders need appropriate discipleship training and mentoring for further spiritual transformation and multiplication among themselves. Parenting skills, marriage enrichment, biblical gender equality and Christian life issues could be a core part of discipleship training for the next generation of leaders.

Education and the Asian Church's Responsibility

> An intelligent heart acquires knowledge,
> and the ear of the wise seeks knowledge. (Prov 18:15)

Education is valued highly among Asians. Secular education is not enough for emerging Asian Christian women servant-leaders. All of these ten women availed themselves of some form of theological/biblical education, with some investing in formal theological training.

The Value of Education for Female Children

All of the Asian Christian women servant-leaders in this book were given or had the opportunity to further themselves with education; some went on to pursue graduate or postgraduate degrees in later years. Realistically, not all Asian children have the option of such planned education. There are agencies like UNICEF and international non-profit organizations addressing this issue as best they can. The governments of these Asian nations also have a vested interest, but there is a need for Christ-centered values in schools. Only Christian agencies and individuals are able to offer this moral encouragement. The churches of Asia and Christian mission agencies have a tremendous responsibility to ensure that every child in Asia has access to education at least to college level.

The Asian Church needs to look further into helping its own children, especially those in poor nations, to secure an education while influencing them with godly values. While some churches are already doing this, more can be done. It is not enough to be dependent on Asian governments – most of whom do not hold to Christian values – to provide solutions. The Asian Church needs to believe that it is strong enough to build schools and offer a viable education to the people. The Asian Church has the capability of being a peace-oriented counter force in the area of education and to stand in opposition to education that teaches hatred, anti-Semitism and false courage (cowardice) in acts of terrorism.

The pursuit of unity, a valuable leadership quality, will be exemplified when Asian churches come together to offer both secular and biblical education for every child without prejudice.

The Value of Theological or Biblical Training for Emerging Asian Christian Women Servant-Leaders

Non-formal training has its place in the church environment. In the last fifteen years of discipling pastors and church leaders, I have noted that a majority of Asian churches are not engaged in intentional discipling. This form of discipling is valuable for new believers who need an assurance of salvation and to learn to practice basic spiritual disciplines. A majority of Asian Christian women servant-leaders are likely to be homemakers or workers on farms or in factories. Each woman is entitled to know with certainty that she is loved by Jesus, is God's child and has a godly purpose in her life. The important realization and understanding that no one has automatic membership of the kingdom of God, just through being born in a Christian family or attending church regularly, would be a basic step to freedom in Christ.

Asian churches, regardless of their congregation sizes, need encouragement to embrace formal, informal or non-formal theological/biblical training as part of their spiritual chromosome. Extending this opportunity for equipping to others who have not had this opportunity yet is worthwhile. One note of caution is that a knowledge-based Christian woman should not be the product. Instead, a wisdom-based Christian woman will affect and impact the kingdom of God in a greater way as she exercises the knowledge gained through obedience.

If Asian Christian women servant-leaders as well as others will invest their time in theological or biblical education, Christianity in Asia will be more dynamic. Asia will not boast of being home to a high percentage of pagan religions but will be able to represent Christ genuinely. It is only through the knowledge and understanding of scriptural teaching that Asian Christian women servant-leaders can step forward to serve God.

Biblical education interests me personally and is a focus of my ministry to men and women globally. The ten narratives are a strong encouragement for me to continue to bring informal theological/biblical and practical ministry training to both men and women within the twenty- to forty-years age group. In my ministry travels I have noted that Asian Christians are hungry and willing to be equipped for ministry but often do not have the financial means to engage in the equipping. Wealthier Asian churches can be encouraged to take on this responsibility to help poor and growing churches.

I have also found that some non-Asian mission agencies provide a modified or easier version of biblical education to women. Personally, I find this an insult to the intelligence of Asian women regardless of their social backgrounds. My own experience has been to teach women (urban and rural) the same course material available to Christian men. Everyone is treated equally, with no exceptions.

The Reality of Persecution in Asia

Persecution is a term that conjures up ideas of physical abuse – beatings, whippings and bodily abuse of all kinds. However, in the narratives, persecution was related to mental and emotional abuse in varying degrees as most of these women went through periods of rejection, low self-esteem and struggles as they stepped into their positions to serve as leaders. Clinton categorizes such times as the ministry-maturing phase.[1] The reality in Asia is that any Christian leader must be prepared for physical, mental and emotional abuse. Mental and emotional abuse is the immediate reality, and may be classified as a form of persecution from within the Church for emerging and current Asian Christian women servant-leaders who are not accepted on equal terms in ministry due to their gender.

While maturing Christians will joyfully count such abuse as trials that perfect their character (Jas 1:2–4), the Asian Church has a serious responsibility not to be a proponent of such mistreatment of gifted and godly women. The plea is repeated to the Asian Church to carefully consider the scriptural teachings regarding women and women in Christian leadership.

Christian Leadership According to the Narratives

The perspectives of Christian leadership according to Asian Christian women servant-leaders include the definition and principles of Christian servant-leadership. The women affected by both cultural and theological interpretations of women and women in leadership cry out for equality in servant-leadership.

Definition, Principles and Equality in Servant-Leadership

In my previous chapter, I entered into a discussion of how the Christian leadership values espoused by Western male leaders are values that are also fully accepted by Asian Christian women. However, Asian Christian women servant-leaders may understand and express these values in a different manner. *The women's collective voice in this book is loud and clear:* We want biblical equality in servant-leadership. We desire to be recognized for our gifts and ministerial contributions on an equal basis with other leaders, both male and female. We are interested in practical, missional engagement with other leaders regardless of gender or theological perspectives.

Most of these women engaged in theological or biblical training during their middle or later years, proving their lifelong learning attitudes. They were keen to move people towards Christ. Simultaneously, these women struggled

---

1. Clinton, *The Making*, 153–166.

to be accepted as servant-leaders. Some cultures identified their women as helpers to male leaders. These women needed to permit themselves to find their security and significance as servant-leaders in Christ. According to the narratives, an appropriate definition of Christian leadership could be:

> Biblical leadership is a lifelong learning process of becoming self-sacrificial, responsible and influential so that more people can be mobilized and impacted for our Lord Jesus Christ, and it is accessible for both men and women.

This definition aims at four principles of servant-leadership:

- *Principle 1: Patience and Perseverance* – Christian leadership is a lifelong learning process.
- *Principle 2: Excellence and Effectiveness* – Christian leadership is a responsible stewardship of gifts and blessings to be shared with all who need them.
- *Principle 3: Vision* – Christian leadership is visionary in submission to God and aims at mobilizing people towards Christ through creative and influential strategies.
- *Principle 4: Equality and Justice* – Christian leadership is fair and equally available to both men and women regardless of cultural, social or theological contexts.

This definition and the four principles will be important in helping emerging Asian Christian women servant-leaders to identify their call and vision for life and ministry.

On a personal note, I am committed to teaching biblical equality in leadership to both men and women. I encourage the Asian Church to explore further these principles of leadership for Asian Christian women and determine if these principles form the heart of leadership among their women.

The Challenge for Asian Women in Servant-Leadership

Asian culture generally dictates that women are placed at a lower level than men. Many women leaders may be as responsible as men in their service in God's kingdom but may not be recognized accordingly. Pastor Elizabeth rose against all the cultural odds to be ordained and was appointed to various leadership positions in her denomination. RA found a creative way around these environments. She accepted the cultural-theological environment that prohibited women from being leaders over men but she became a servant-leader for Arab women in the region. Young Kim remained passive-assertive; she was passive with her voice but assertive in her actions to see God's call in her life being fulfilled.

The ten narratives reveal that Asian Christian women are called to be godly, lifelong disciples of Christ, visionaries and change agents for their families, churches and communities. Pursuing God and being available to him matters – age, marital status and nationality did not stop these women from being creative in their growth as servant-leaders. In this journey, they made an impact on the lives of both men and women. They worked hard to remain in unity with male leaders.

Asian Christian women servant-leaders who have experienced various challenges to their leadership need to encourage Asian Christian men and women to raise their standards of biblical leadership and to understand that servant-leadership is deeply sacrificial for both genders.

Raising the Standard for Asian Christian Men

Asian Christian women servant-leaders have been able to succeed and grow strong in ministries despite many challenges because they had male encouragers who motivated them with verbal encouragements, prayer and moral support, role modeled Christian godliness, disciplines or behavior, or even mentored them. For those who are married, their spouses were their best encouragers and cheerleaders. Still, there is room for improvement among Christian male leaders to learn to encourage their female counterparts.

Culturally, Asian men are not prone to providing encouragement; thus, educating Asian Christian male leaders to offer biblical encouragement to female leaders would free the Asian Church from this cultural stronghold. While co-educational classes may already be offered in Asian seminaries or churches, Asian Christian male leaders need to learn the importance of the encouragement of women within their cultural-theological contexts. One suggestion from the narratives is that co-educational classes held to enable both Christian men and women to know and understand the issues and struggles would be helpful for both parties.

Raising the Standard for Asian Christian Women

Except for RA, who is bound by cultural, gender and theological contextual challenges, all the other women have had experience of ministering as leaders to both men and women. The other nine women did the work of pastors, teachers, counselors and evangelists but lacked appropriate recognition. They do not receive any wages for their service because they are volunteers. Moreover, some of these women are theologically trained and producing spiritual children regionally, if not internationally. If an Asian Christian male leader were in a similar situation, he would be recognized, appointed a key church leader and perhaps be ordained as a pastor.

One thing that the ten Asian Christian women proved was that, by God's abundant grace, they were able to rise up as servant-leaders who obeyed the Great Commission. These women share the whole gamut of ministries: pioneers of church plants, non-profit agencies and fellowships; disciple-makers; producers of future pastors and missionaries; author; Bible teachers; and evangelists, pastors, missionaries and intercessors.

This provides a strong encouragement that, given the appropriate cross-cultural training and opportunities, one Asian Christian woman servant-leader can impact hundreds now and thousands in the future; ten such women can do much more.[2] I suggest that Asian churches recognize the potential of this large "unreached"[3] group within Asia with a sense of urgency and begin to invest in evangelizing and producing more godly ministers for these times.

In my ministry, I intend to challenge Asian pastors and leaders to exercise fairness and offer due recognition to women who are performing leadership responsibilities just like their fellow Christian brothers. However, the issue of gender inequality needs to be approached within the bigger context of educating pastors and leaders about leadership with love and humility.

Sacrificial Christian Leadership

All Christian leaders regardless of gender are expected to offer sacrificial service for kingdom purposes. This sacrifice ultimately lends itself to mobilization of people for and toward Christ. This sacrifice is meant for both men and women; there is no difference. The study revealed that Asian Christian women – all of whom come from nations which are patriarchal in nature – desired more equality in Christian leadership. Until equality in Christian leadership becomes

---

2. In this study, I did not attempt to calculate the number of lives these ten women have collectively touched. However, it is evident from the scope of their ministries that the ten women will have touched over a hundred lives. For example, RA's engagement with Arab women is not localized but extends from her nation to the other seventeen Arab nations. Another example is Kat, who has been travelling for more than twenty years to teach pastors, leaders and others in other nations.

3. By "unreached" in this context, I refer to the larger female population in Asia comprising both Christians and potential Christians.

a true reality in Asia, "true Christian leadership does not exist," according to RA, a Jordanian.

The voices are crying out to the Asian Church to reflect on the type of theological and cultural environment that is being established for current and emerging Asian Christian women servant-leaders. Does this environment nourish and nurture their women to become strong servant-leaders in God's kingdom, or are these women sidelined to remain as cheerleaders and supporters? Is the Asian Church's leadership simply telling women what to do, or is it allowing godly women to come alongside in leadership and partnership? When an Asian church invites a formerly suppressed Muslim woman to become a Christian, will this suppression be extended by limiting the new Muslim-background believer in her rise as a servant-leader for Christ within her church? Will her male Christian leaders welcome her thoughtful perspectives? These are questions that the Asian Church needs to ponder and explore for the sake of empowering Asian Christian women.

Role Modeling and Mentoring

Christ-like character and spiritual disciplines exercised by encouragers, both men and women, affected these ten Asian Christian women in their leadership journey. Both gender groups are capable of bringing their faith experiences and expertise to nourish the growth of Asian Christian women. When such freedom within the boundaries of accountability is exercised, women servant-leaders also begin to be freed to embody the learning from both parties. They will likely pass on this learning to other men and women. Engaging with both men and women encouragers who are also consistent in exercising the spiritual disciplines of prayer, fellowship and service can only be beneficial for the growth of women servant-leaders.

Since opposite-sex interactions may cause anxiety to some Asian churches, they could explore the comfort levels of such encouragers and work within their comfort levels or established boundaries. I have found that such interactions are possible when one truly is able to view the other person as a child of God. It boils down to who we are in Christ. In my ministry, I am extremely thankful to the many Christian brothers in Africa, Asia, the Americas and Europe who have accompanied me from location to location for ministry purposes. It is certainly possible to work alongside brothers without feeling guilty about being a female, or at times the only female in the group.

The Asian Church's Responsibility in Creatively Communicating the Gospel

The narratives inform us that most of the women encountered Christ through pulpit and fellowship ministries. A combination of the strong and response-seeking proclamation of the gospel, coupled with the love and care of a dynamic fellowship, would be effective in increasing the Asian Church population. It must be noted that some Asian churches are engaging in this strategy to win souls. However, the proclamation of the gospel must be clear and the hearer of the gospel must be able to understand the doctrines of salvation.

In my ministry, I have learned not to assume that worshippers fully understand the doctrine of salvation or are fully assured of their salvation. In my own testimony, I did not understand the things of God until I was discipled in my adult years.

The Asian Church has a strong responsibility to ensure that every believer is equipped to creatively communicate the gospel to an unbeliever. It would benefit the new believer to enjoy basic discipleship training with an encourager who will walk alongside him or her for a period of time. Again, it must be noted that some churches are already offering this basic equipping, but it is not sufficient as the Asian Church is not running at full strength; otherwise we might witness an exponential increase among our membership.

Conclusion

There is an available task force[4] for the expansion of God's kingdom and there is a sense of urgency for the Asian Church to recognize and adopt this task force. In order to mobilize this major task force, it is necessary for the twenty-first-century church leadership to better equip current and emerging Asian Christian women servant-leaders. They must be nurtured and nourished in a suitable theological and cultural environment. Asian Christian leaders, both men and women, have a serious responsibility to accelerate discipleship, multiply servant-leaders and work together as equals in the kingdom of God.

Recently, I wrote the following short lament as part of a trauma healing session. I began to realize that my own trauma was related to how women were viewed as Christian leaders.

---

4. The "task force" of women refers to both pre-believers and current believers.

When women who hope in Christ
are criticized and their service in leadership is mocked,
their God-given gifts stripped away, unused,
by brothers and sisters in Christ,
a great divide happens in the body of Christ.

The divide that should not be,
no, not in the body of Christ,
where there should be perfect unity,
a kingdom mindset that embraces
women in servant-leadership,
where arrogance is crushed
and humility is birthed again.

But the current sin in man
screams otherwise:
competition, incompetence, threats, never as good as the man in
    leadership –
all words of shame
released to down-size the woman
who desires to serve her own people,
who desires to serve her God.

So, here's my hope in a great God
who loves both men and women equally,
that by the blood shed by his Son,
there will be a return of true unity.

The body of Christ in perfect motion,
men and women living and believing in equality.
Thank you, God, that you show us the unity through Christ.
You can bring back this sanity to our humanity.

It is my personal prayer that there will be an influx of Asian Christian women servant-leaders rising up to make Christ known among the nations, in God's power and grace. It is also my prayer that no Christian woman will be ashamed of her God-given leadership gifting or her intention to work in unity with her brother(s) in Christ. May God raise up a mighty force of Asian Christian women servant-leaders for the expansion of his kingdom and for his glory.

References

Ahmed, Leila. *Women and Gender in Islam*. New Haven: Yale University Press, 1992.

Associated Press. "Body of a Woman Who Was Gang-Raped on a Bus in New Delhi Is Cremated in a Private Ceremony." *Fox News* online, 30 December 2012. http://www.foxnews.com/world/2012/12/30/body-woman-who-was-gang-raped-on-bus-in-new-delhi-is-cremated-in-private/. Accessed 5 February 2013.

Athyal, Saphir. "Toward an Asian Christian Theology." In *The Bible and Theology in Asian Contexts*, edited by Bong Rin Ro and Ruth Eshenaur, 11, 50–52. Taichung, Taiwan: ATA, 1984.

Australian Government: National Health and Medical Research Council. *National Statement on Ethical Conduct in Human Research (2007) – Updated May 2015*. https://www.nhmrc.gov.au/guidelines-publications/e72. Accessed 16 July 2013.

Barna, George. *A Fish Out of Water*. Nashville: Integrity Publishers, 2002.

Bernard, H. Russell. *Research Methods in Anthropology*. 3rd edition. Walnut Creek, CA: AltaMira Press, 2001.

Blackaby, Henry T., and Richard Blackaby. *Spiritual Leadership*. Nashville, TN: B&H, 2011.

Burns, Robert B. *Introduction to Research Methods*. 4th ed. Thousand Oaks, CA: Sage, 2000.

Center for Asia-Pacific Women in Politics. "Women Heads of State." 4 March 2009. http://www.capwip.org/participation/womenheadofstate.html. Accessed 17 September 2012.

Chakkalakal, Pauline. "Asian Women Reshaping Theology: Challenges and Hopes." *Feminist Theology: The Journal of the Britain and Ireland School of Feminist Theology* 9, no. 27 (May 2001): 21–35. Database: Academic Search Premier. Accessed 7 March 2014 from Ebscohost.

Chan, Jasmine. "The Status of Women in a Patriarchal State: The Case of Singapore." In *Women in Asia*, edited by Louise Edwards and Mina Roces, 39–58. New South Wales, Australia: Asian Studies Association of Australia, 2000.

Chan, Simon. *Spiritual Theology*. Downers Grove, IL: InterVarsity Press, 1998.

Chaudhry, Serena. "Millions Pushed into Child Labor in Pakistan." *Reuters*, 7 February 2012. http://www.reuters.com/article/2012/02/07/pakistan-childlabour-idUSL4E8D63H620120207. Accessed 17 September 2012.

Christian Conference of Asia. "Mission in Unity and Contextual Theology." cca.org.hk/home/mission-in-unity-and-contextual-theology/. Accessed 12 March 2016.

Chung, Sook-Ja. "Women Church in Korea: Voices and Visions." *Ecumenical Review* 53, no. 1 (Jan 2001): 72–81. Database: Academic Search Premier. Accessed 7 March 2014 from Ebscohost.

Clinton, Robert J. *The Making of a Leader*. Singapore: Navigators, 1988.

————. *The Making of a Leader*. 2nd ed. Colorado Springs, CO: NavPress, 2012.

Clinton, Robert J., and Richard W. Clinton. *Unlocking Your Giftedness*. Altadena, CA: Barnabas, 1993.

Cochran, Pamela D. H. *Evangelical Feminism*. New York: New York University Press, 2005.

"Confucian Inspired Sayings." *WomenInWorldHistory.com*. http://www. womeninworldhistory.com/lesson3plus.html. Accessed 16 November 2010.

Cranfield, C. E. B. *A Critical and Exegetical Commentary on the Epistle to the Romans*, Vol. 1. International Critical Commentary on the Holy Scriptures of the Old and New Testaments, edited by J. A. Emerton and C. E. B. Cranfield. Edinburgh: T&T Clark, 1977.

Cunningham, Loren, and David L. Hamilton. *Why Not Women?* Seattle: YWAM, 2000.

De Pree, Max. *Leadership Is an Art*. New York: Random House, 2004.

"The Dowry Prohibition Act, 1961." *Vakilno1.com*. http://www.vakilno1.com/bareacts/dowryprohibitionact/s1.html. Accessed 25 November 2012.

Dunn, James D. G. *Romans 1–8*. Word Biblical Commentary 38A. Dallas: Word, 1988.

Ebry, Patricia. *Chinese Civilization: A Sourcebook*. New York: Free Press, 1993.

Edwards, Louise, and Mina Roces, eds. *Women in Asia*. New South Wales, Australia: Asian Studies Association of Australia, 2000.

Einhorn, Bruce. "Innovation: Singapore Is No. 1, Well Ahead of the U.S." *Bloomberg*, 16 March 2009. https://www.bloomberg.com/news/articles/2009-03-16/innovation-singapore-is-no-dot-1-well-ahead-of-the-u-dot-s. Accessed 15 September 2012.

Fee, Gordon D. "The Priority of Spirit Gifting for Church Ministry." In *Discovering Biblical Equality*, edited by Ronald W. Pierce, Rebecca M. Groothuis and Gordon D. Fee, 241. Grand Rapids, MI: Baker, 2005.

Gajiwala, Astrid Lobo. "Power Struggles: In God's Image." Cited in "Asian Women Reshaping Theology: Challenges and Hopes," by Pauline Chakkalakal. *Feminist Theology: The Journal of the Britain and Ireland School of Feminist Theology* 9, no. 27 (May 2001). Database: Academic Search Premier. Accessed 7 March 2014 from Ebsco Host.

Glanville, Elizabeth. "Leadership Development for Women in Ministry." PhD thesis, Fuller Theological Seminary, 2000.

Gnanakan, Ken, ed. *Biblical Theology in Asia*. Bangalore: Theological Book Trust, 1995.

Goh, Robbie B. H. "Christian Identities in Singapore: Religion, Race and Culture between State Controls and Transnational Flows." *Journal of Cultural Geography* 26, no. 1 (Feb 2009). Database: GALE|A197925754.

Greenleaf, Robert. *The Institution as Servant*. Westfield, IN: Robert K. Greenleaf Center, 2009.

————. *The Servant as Leader*. Westfield, IN: Robert K. Greenleaf Center, 2008.

Grenz, Stanley. *Revisioning Evangelical Theology: A Fresh Agenda for the 21st Century.* Downers Grove, IL: InterVarsity Press, 1993.

Groothuis, Rebecca M. *Good News for Women: A Biblical Picture of Gender Equality.* Grand Rapids, MI: Baker, 1997.

Gulshan, Esther, and Thelma Sangster. *The Torn Veil.* Grand Rapids, MI: Zondervan, 2004.

Haggai, John. *The Influential Leader.* Eugene, OR: Harvest House, 2009.

Hamilton, David J. "Jesus Broke Down the Walls." In *Why Not Women?*, edited by Loren Cunningham and David L. Hamilton, 127. Seattle: YWAM, 2000.

Hassey, Janette. "Evangelical Women in Ministry a Century Ago: The Early 19th and 20th Centuries." In *Discovering Biblical Equality*, edited by Ronald W. Pierce, Rebecca M. Groothuis and Gordon D. Fee, 39–57. Grand Rapids, MI: Baker, 2005.

Higham, Kevin. "Questioning the Question!" *Evangel* 21, no. 3 (Autumn 2003): 89.

Hnuni, R. L. "Contextualizing Asian Theologies: Women's Perspectives." *Asian Journal of Theology* 18, no. 1 (April 2004): 138–145.

Holland, Kelley. "Office Space: Under New Management – How Diversity Makes a Team Click." *New York Times* online, 22 April 2007. http://query.nytimes.com/gst/fullpage.html?res=9D07E1DC163EF931A15757C0A9619C8B63. Accessed 13 November 2012.

Horan, Jane. "How to Retain and Develop Asian Women Leaders." *Business Week*, 7 November 2009. http://www.businessweek.com/stories/2009-11-06/how-to-retain-and-develop-asian-women-leadersbusinessweek-business-news-stock-market-and-financial-advice. Accessed 11 July 2013.

Hunt, Susan, and Peggy Hutcheson. *Leadership for Women in the Church.* Grand Rapids, MI: Zondervan, 1991.

Isherwood, Lisa, and Dorothea McEwan. *Introducing Feminist Theology.* 2nd edition. Sheffield: Sheffield Academic Press, 2001.

Jin, Yong Ting. "On Being Church: Asian Women's Voices and Visions." *Ecumenical Review* 53, no. 1 (Jan 2001): 109–113. Database: Academic Search Premier. Accessed 7 March 2014 from Ebscohost.

Joshua Project. "What Is the 10/40 Window?" http://www.joshuaproject.net. Accessed 13 October 2012.

Kim, Young S. *The King's Invitation.* Seoul: Duranno, 2011.

Kim, Youngmin, and Michael J. Pettid, eds. *Women and Confucianism in Chosŏn Korea: New Perspectives.* New York: State University of New York, 2011.

Kroeger, Richard Clark, and Catherine Clark Kroeger. *I Suffer Not a Woman.* 6th ed. Grand Rapids, MI: Baker, 2003.

LaCugna, Catherine M. *God for Us: The Trinity and Christian Life.* New York: Harper, 1993.

Le Peau, Andrew T. "The High Cost of Leadership." http://www.intervarsity.org/slj/wi89/wi89_high_cost_of_leadership.html. Accessed 23 November 2012.

Malphurs, Aubrey. "Growing Leaders for Ministry in the 21st Century." *Enrichment Journal*. http://enrichmentjournal.ag.org/200601/200601_050_GrowLeaders.cfm. Accessed 12 November 2012.

Marczyk, Geoffrey R., David DeMatteo and David Festinger. *Essentials of Research Design and Methodology*. Hoboken, NJ: John Wiley & Sons, 2005.

Maxwell, L. E. *Women in Ministry*. Camp Hill, PA: Christian Publications, 1987.

McCullum, Garrett. "VCs Say Singapore's the Best Hub for Asia Investments." *VentureBeat*, 28 September 2010. http://venturebeat.com/2010/09/28/vcs-say-singapores-the-best-hub-for-asia-investments/. Accessed 15 September 2012.

Moffett, Sam Hugh. *A History of Christianity in Asia*. Vol. 1: *Beginnings to 1500*. San Francisco: Harper & Row, 1992.

Moore, Carol. "Quotes from M. K. Gandhi." *CarolMoore.net*. http://www.carolmoore. net/articles/gandhi-quotes.html. Accessed 29 November 2010.

Mounce, Robert H., and William D. Mounce, *The Mounce Reverse-Interlinear™ New Testament* (MOUNCE) Copyright © 2011. *BibleGateway.com*. http://www. biblegateway.com/passage/?search=Romans+8%3A30-32&version=MOUNCE. Accessed 3 January 2014.

Panagoda, Charundi. "Global Gender Imbalance Poses Critical Problems for Women." *GlobalIssues.org*, 21 February 2012. http://www.globalissues.org/news/2012/02/21/12798. Accessed 13 October 2012.

Park, Bokyoung. "The Contribution of Korean Christian Women to the Church and Its Mission: Implications for an Evangelical Missiology." PhD thesis, Fuller Theological Seminary, 1999.

Pickthall, Marmaduke William. *The Meaning of the Glorious Qur'an*. Bombay: Government Central Press, 1938.

———. "Feminism and Missiology." In *Footprints of God*, edited by Charles Van Engen, Thomas Nancy and Gallagher Robert. Monrovia, CA: MARC, 1999.

Pierce, Ronald W. "Contemporary Evangelicals for Gender Equality." In *Discovering Biblical Equality*, edited by Ronald W. Pierce, Rebecca M. Groothuis and Gordon D. Fee, 58. Grand Rapids, MI: Baker, 2005.

Pierce, Ronald W., Rebecca M. Groothuis and Gordon D. Fee, eds. *Discovering Biblical Equality*. Grand Rapids, MI: Baker, 2005.

Piper, John, and Wayne Grudem. *Recovering Biblical Manhood and Womanhood: A Response to Evangelical Feminism*. Wheaton, IL: Crossway, 1991.

Prasso, Sheridan. "Spas Take Off in Asia." 21 August 2009. http://money.cnn. com/2009/08/20/news/international/spas_asia_boom.fortune/index.htm. Accessed 14 September 2012.

Ramabai, Pandita. *An Autobiography of Pandita Ramabai: Woman of the Millennium*. New Delhi: Genesis Publishers, 2008.

Riessman, Catherine Kohler. *Narrative Analysis*. Newberry Park, CA: Sage, 1993.

Riswold, Caryn D. *Feminism and Christianity*. Eugene, OR: Cascade, 2009.

Ro, Bong Rin. "Contextualization: Asian Theology." In *The Bible and Theology in Asian Contexts*, edited by Bong Rin Ro and Ruth Eshenaur, 73. Taichung, Taiwan: ATA, 1984.

Ro, Bong Rin, and Ruth Eshenaur, eds. *The Bible and Theology in Asian Contexts*. Taichung, Taiwan: ATA, 1984.

Roces, Mina, and Louise Edwards. "Contesting Gender Narratives, 1970–2000." In *Women in Asia*, edited by Mina Roces and Louise Edwards, 10–15. New South Wales, Australia: Asian Studies Association of Australia, 2000.

Rosenlee, Lisa Li-Hsiang. *Confucianism and Women: A Philosophical Interpretation*. New York: State University of New York Press, 2006.

Rosenwald, G. C., and R. L. Ochberg, eds. *Storied Lives: The Cultural Politics of Self-Understanding*. New Haven, CT: Yale University, 1992.

Ryrie, Charles. *Basic Theology*. Chicago: Moody, 1999.

Sanders, J. Oswald. *Spiritual Leadership*. Chicago: Moody, 1994.

Shingh, Kamayani. "The Dowry System and Women in India." 2005. http://subsite.icu.ac.jp/cgs/article/0408008e.html. Accessed 25 May 2011.

Smith, Mark K. "What Is Non-Formal Education?" *Infed.org*, 2001. http://infed.org/mobi/what-is-non-formal-education/. Accessed 3 July 2012.

Stableford, Dylan. "Malala Yousafzai Speaks Publicly for First Time since Taliban Shooting." *Yahoo! News*, 4 February 2013. http://news.yahoo.com/blogs/lookout/malala-yousafzai-speaks-video-143346420.html. Accessed 4 February 2013.

Stivens, Maila. "Becoming Modern in Malaysia: Women at the End of the Twentieth Century." In *Women in Asia*, edited by Mina Roces and Louise Edwards, 16–28. New South Wales, Australia: Asian Studies Association of Australia, 2000.

Strong's Greek Concordance. http://biblehub.com/greek/1249.htm.

Swindoll, Charles R. "The Rewards of a Life Well-Lived." *Christian Leadership Alliance*. http://ym.christianleadershipalliance.org/?page=LifeWellLived. Accessed 23 November 2012.

Tano, Rodrigo D. "Toward an Evangelical Theology." In *The Bible and Theology in Asian Contexts*, edited by Bong Rin Ro and Ruth Eshenaur, 99. Taichung, Taiwan: ATA, 1984.

Transparency International. "Corruption Perceptions Index 2011." http://cpi.transparency.org/cpi2011/results/. Accessed 16 September 2012.

UNESCO Institute for Statistics. *Global Education Digest 2010: Comparing Education Statistics around the World*. Quebec: UNESCO Institute for Statistics, 2010. http://www.uis.unesco.org/Library/Documents/GED_2010_EN.pdf. Accessed 20 June 2012.

Unger, Merrill F. *The New Unger's Bible Dictionary*. Chicago: Moody, 1988.

UN-Habitat. "Asia Pacific Ministerial Conference on Housing and Human Settlements." 2006. http://www.unhabitat.org/content.asp?cid=4202&catid=643&typeid=46. Accessed 13 July 2013.

UNICEF South Asia. "Protection of Children from Violence, Abuse and Exploitation." http://www.unicef.org/rosa/protection.html. Accessed 13 October 2012.

United Nations ESCAP. *2016 ESCAP Population Data Sheet.* 29 September 2016. http://www.unescap.org/resources/2016-escap-population-data-sheet. Accessed 9 February 2017.

United Nations Population Division. "WPP2015 POP F01 3 Total Population – Female." Department of Economic and Social Affairs. 2015. https://esa.un.org/unpd/wpp/Download/Standard/Population/. Accessed 14 February 2017.

United States Census Bureau. 2016. http://www.census.gov/programs-surveys/popest.html. Accessed 9 February 2016.

Uy, Veronica. "Trafficking of Filipinas in Singapore 'Unabated' – Says Embassy." *Global Nation Inquirer,* 28 April 2008. http://globalnation.inquirer.net/news/breakingnews/view/20080428-133194/Trafficking-of-Filipinas-in-Singapore-unabated--embassy. Accessed 17 September 2012.

Valea, Ernest. "Salvation and Eternal Life in World Religions." *ComparativeReligion.com.* http://www.comparativereligion.com/salvation.html#01. Accessed 24 November 2012.

The Voice of the Martyrs. "Restricted Nations." http://www.persecution.com/public/nationsdefined.aspx?clickfrom=c2lkZWJhcg%3D%3D. Accessed 28 November 2012.

Watson, Natalie K. *Feminist Theology.* Grand Rapids, MI: Eerdmans, 2003.

Webster, Leonard, and Patricie Mertova. *Using Narrative Inquiry as a Research Method: An Introduction to Using Critical Event Narrative Analysis in Research on Learning and Teaching.* New York: Routledge, 2007.

White, John. *The Fight.* Reprint. Leicester: InterVarsity Press, 1996.

Wilkes, Gene C. *Jesus on Leadership.* Wheaton, IL: Tyndale House, 1998.

The World Bank. "Population, Female (% of Total)." http://data.worldbank.org/indicator/SP.POP.TOTL.FE.ZS/countries/1W?display=map. Accessed 7 May 2013.

Langham Literature and its imprints are a ministry of Langham Partnership.

Langham Partnership is a global fellowship working in pursuit of the vision God entrusted to its founder John Stott –

to facilitate the growth of the church in maturity and Christ-likeness through raising the standards of biblical preaching and teaching.

Our vision is to see churches in the majority world equipped for mission and growing to maturity in Christ through the ministry of pastors and leaders who believe, teach and live by the Word of God.

Our mission is to strengthen the ministry of the Word of God through:
• nurturing national movements for biblical preaching
• fostering the creation and distribution of evangelical literature
• enhancing evangelical theological education
especially in countries where churches are under-resourced.

Our ministry

Langham Preaching partners with national leaders to nurture indigenous biblical preaching movements for pastors and lay preachers all around the world. With the support of a team of trainers from many countries, a multi-level programme of seminars provides practical training, and is followed by a programme for training local facilitators. Local preachers' groups and national and regional networks ensure continuity and ongoing development, seeking to build vigorous movements committed to Bible exposition.

Langham Literature provides majority world preachers, scholars and seminary libraries with evangelical books and electronic resources through publishing and distribution, grants and discounts. The programme also fosters the creation of indigenous evangelical books in many languages, through writer's grants, strengthening local evangelical publishing houses, and investment in major regional literature projects, such as one volume Bible commentaries like *The Africa Bible Commentary* and *The South Asia Bible Commentary.*

Langham Scholars provides financial support for evangelical doctoral students from the majority world so that, when they return home, they may train pastors and other Christian leaders with sound, biblical and theological teaching. This programme equips those who equip others. Langham Scholars also works in partnership with majority world seminaries in strengthening evangelical theological education. A growing number of Langham Scholars study in high quality doctoral programmes in the majority world itself. As well as teaching the next generation of pastors, graduated Langham Scholars exercise significant influence through their writing and leadership.

To learn more about Langham Partnership and the work we do visit **langham.org**

CPSIA information can be obtained
at www.ICGtesting.com
Printed in the USA
BVHW09s2022241018
531126BV00015B/65/P

9 781783 683666